Better Than We Believed
2

Better Than We Believed 2

Where Jesus and the Church Fit In

Robert J. Cormier

✝

A Crossroad Book
The Crossroad Publishing Company
New York

The Crossroad Publishing Company
www.CrossroadPublishing.com

© 2018 by Robert J. Cormier

ISBN 978-0-8245-2193-6

Library of Congress Cataloging-in-Publication Data available from the Library of Congress.

Cover design by George Foster

ISBN 978-0-8245-8992-9 (epub)

◘

CONTENTS

■

INTRODUCTION

As a visiting presenter, Father Mike had once given a talk entitled "Faith: We Have It Backward!" His grand goal had been to give people the idea that faith is "vision."

Faith, he had said, is about seeing the deep meaning of things and letting what we see lead to a concrete and wonderful explanation—one that dramatically changes how we view life, death, and every situation.

This, he explained, is the true "power" of faith. Seeing things with the vision that is faith, we receive the "gifts of faith," the effects on our spirits that automatically follow because of what we see. Father Mike had not wanted to complicate things too much by going on to explain where Jesus and the Church fit in. That would be the topic of a new talk at another time.

Well, the time had come; and this time his goal was not only to explain where Jesus and the Church fit in, but also to give people the special encouragements that God intended when He sent Jesus to be born poor, suffer much, die brutally, and share one last supper with his disciples before his death.

As (almost) always, Father Mike's talks would inspire (or provoke) people to make appointments.

In this book, the seven people you will meet are coming to Father Mike with, broadly speaking, two different motives. Four represent areas in which traditional Catholics or other conservative Christians might find fault with the ideas proposed here as a faith that can make sense to the future, a future that has already begun.

Three others embody moral issues. Certainly, any set of ideas proposing to call itself "the faith of the future" must be able to make a sensible response to questions of right and wrong that impact the lives of almost everyone.

Besides this, we will hear a homily by Father Mike that aims to explain certain practical principles that have their basis in the future's faith—and want to help us get there.

Finally, Father Mike will meet someone who will challenge the beautiful-sounding things he tells people about the love of God for everyone, and the role everyone plays in making the family that we will all be in heaven.

Perhaps by being present as these important truths are discussed, you will grow in confidence that we have nothing to fear from the faith of the future—and everything to gain.

Though *Better Than We Believed 2* can be read independently, this book is best read after the first title in the series, *Better Than We Believed.* ∎

PART I:
WHERE JESUS AND
THE CHURCH FIT IN

□

JESUS AND THE CHURCH

Father Mike was smiling. More people had come to his second conference than to the first. This was good; but considering that he had planned this second talk as a continuation of the first, it also meant that he would need to start with a recap of the basic ideas he was planning to build on.

RECAP

"Let's start with what we started with last time," he said. "Let's be clear about the main way we get faith backward."

Some people were hearing this for the first time.

"Far too many people think that 'having faith' means that 'if I *really* believe that God will do this for me, He will do it.'

"And even when you point out to them that God knows what we need better than we do, and because of His love He is always leading us where we need to go ... they agree; but still they say, 'but I *really* believe that God will do this for me.'

"I'm not always sure what people *really* believe," continued Father Mike, "but I do think that people confuse what they *really* believe with what they *really* want.

"This is not the faith of a deep spirit. The faith of a deep spirit knows that God knows better than we do what we need. It understands that sometimes God needs us to go through some hard things *now* in order to give us something much better later. It says 'no' to what we want now and 'yes' to God's greatness and love."

Father Mike continued. "Real faith is about 'vision.'

"It's about looking carefully at things and experiencing that their source is something greater. This some-*thing* is some-*one*. It is God, and God is good, and everything He does, He does for our good.

"Real faith is not at all troubled by questions of 'proof.'

"It is happy that 'seeing is believing' because what faith sees when it looks at the world is God standing behind it.

"It knows that as we grow ... which means becoming more developed 'inside' ... we come to see God better and better.

"Faith knows that this is what we are doing here in this world—growing into knowing our Maker, and getting ready to share His life forever.

"It is plain to see," said Father Mike, "we were *NOT* made to live our lives here and come to nothing. God would not have given us life so He could take life away. No, we were made for life, life with God forever. We call this 'heaven.'

"We are here, in this world, before we go to heaven so that God in His goodness can give us *more*— the chance to become people that *we* helped make, so that we could become our own persons, because it is better for us if we are.

"And how do we do this?" asked Father Mike. But this was not a question. "We do it by growing— by growing in the love that makes us more like God. The point is to understand Him better, so that when we see Him face-to-face, we can share His life more richly forever.

"So, heaven, love ... and that third basic we talked about last time: God works with us through everything He sends into our lives, according to His plan for all things. He sends these *knowing how we will respond*. This way He gets us to become the people *He* wants us to be, people He knows He will love with all His heart forever—and, at the same time, we do the work and become people that *we* made. This, we saw, is the doctrine of God's plan. And we also saw that if we believe in God's plan, our lives are changed. We see what happens, especially the hard things that happen, differently. We see *ourselves* differently. We get the most precious of 'the gifts of faith.'"

ONCE AGAIN, THE GIFTS OF FAITH

"The gifts of faith ... we talked about these last time, too," said Father Mike.

"The gifts of faith are those wonderful effects on our spirits that automatically follow if we *really* see things in the light of the truth that explains our lives. They are those magnificent effects on our spirits that automatically follow if we *really* see things in terms of heaven, love, and God's plan."

The people who had come for the second time now heard some words that sounded distinctly familiar: "Faith in God's plan lets us love ourselves for the right reason, because God has made us who we are so far.

"We are talking about God, who is infinite and can put all He has into everything He does. He puts all he has into every aspect of His plan for each of us, and this means that He has put His all into His plan for you, and for every other human being. Each one; no exceptions.

"This means no more comparing ourselves to others; they have their roles in making us the family we are going to be in heaven, and we have our roles.

6

God needs us all, each one of us, to play the part that he or she has been given.

"Thanks to faith in God's plan: No more criticizing ourselves for what we cannot yet do or what we have done and cannot change. If there's something we can't yet do, God hasn't let us do it yet. If it is something we've done *and cannot change*, then it's something that needed to happen ... to teach us or to teach somebody else, to affect history.... Either way, God would not have put us here liable to do something we cannot change that could make us sad forever.

"Instead, faith in God's plan lets us be thrilled right now for who we are, and this opens the door to a sincere love for other people.

"Some of you will remember this," said Father Mike. "It's a saying in faith: If you love yourself you will always love others. If you love yourself, you feel good and, automatically, you want to do good—you want to love. This is how our goodness is us being like God.

"But if you do not love yourself, you cannot love others. What, after all, is love? Love is when you see the goodness beyond yourself. But if you don't see the goodness within yourself, the goodness out there will bother you. It will make you feel 'less.' On the other hand, if you do see the goodness within you, then the goodness out there doesn't bother you at all. You are free to see the goodness God put in others and to love, and this is what we are here for.

"Love of self," continued Father Mike, "is the 'first' gift of faith. It's first because it's the most important. It's the most important because without it, happiness and holiness are just not possible."

Father Mike now moved on to gift number two.

"Faith in God's plan allows us to accept *anything* that has happened and cannot be changed. We may not know why something hard had to happen, but we do know that someday, when we find out what God has made from it, we will be thrilled. Likewise," added Father Mike, "to believe in God's plan allows us to accept whatever is happening now and cannot yet be changed.

"Since we know that everything that is going to happen—once it has happened and cannot be changed—will also follow God's plan, we can live our lives without fear. If we know that a year from now we are going to be exactly where God wants us to be, what's to fear? If we think the same about our family and friends, we can live without the impossible burden of thinking that everything depends on us. Everything does not depend on us. Everything depends on God. Our job is to do our best, the best we can right now. The rest is up to God and His plan.

"Faith in love inspires us to do *our* parts. We know why we are here. We know what we should do. We know that what we do will make an eternal difference.

"Let's face it," said Father Mike, "if we believe that we are here to grow in love, we love. We are free to live the only kind of lives that could ever satisfy us.

"Many people *want* to love ... they want to do the right thing ... but they can't, they just *can't*, because they have the fear that they are working harder than other people, sacrificing more, and that this somehow makes them 'fools.'

"*But* if loving, and growing in love, is a richer life *forever*, why should what others are *not* doing stop me?!

"And if I am really doing more than others, doesn't that make what I am doing greater?! Isn't it better if I am the only one who wins the lottery?"

This got a laugh.

"Yes," said Father Mike, "faith frees us to live the only kind of life that can make us happy." Father Mike paused. "God is no fool," he said. "God would not have made us so that we could ever be happy doing what is wrong. Rather, He made us so that we can be happy only when we are doing what is right. This is the reason that if we live selfishly we are never satisfied, no matter how much we have, whereas if we live a life of love we are always satisfied, no matter how little we have.

"If to grow in faith and love is our goal, then we get something that people really want but have come to believe is not possible—*control*, control over our lives. We cannot have control if fame or fortune is our goal. If something worldly is our goal, we have to hope that the world will cooperate. And you know it probably won't; we can't control that! If, instead, to grow in faith and love is our goal, we can always choose what we want: to act with faith and love, no matter what the world may do. If something goes wrong, we can accept it, and thus our faith will still grow. If people offend or disappoint us, we can forgive them, and this way our love will still grow.

"And from faith in heaven we get the most of all.

"Faith in heaven frees us from the dread of death, or the need to keep ourselves distracted—never really living—because we cannot face the fact that we, like all human beings, will someday die.

"Faith in heaven frees us from anguish at the deaths of those we love. Though we may miss them, we know that they have gone to God and are more alive than we are. We also know that one day we will be reunited with them. Knowing that we are not going to lose them, we feel freer to love them while they are here.

"Faith in heaven lets us dream. Though all of us have our dreams, the day comes when most people have to admit, if only to themselves, that their dreams are not going to come true. This never happens to people of faith. We know that our dreams are going to come true, in the only place where they ever could. Our dreams do not mock us, reminding us of what our life is *not*. They give us joy because they give us a glimpse of what is coming, what we *will* have, forever.

"Knowing that we were made for divine life, we understand that we were made to *want* divine life. Presumably we also understand that no worldly possession or person or achievement could ever fill us—to get one thing is to want another. Therefore, though we can and should work to make our lives and our world better, we need not suffer over any one thing we do not yet have. We need not anguish over any one problem we have not yet solved. We need not suffer envy.

"Not seeking more from possessions or people than they can give, we can enjoy the possessions and relationships we do have. Our houses do not have to be heavenly mansions; they are not in heaven. But if we find love in our houses, they can still be our homes. The people in our lives do not need to be perfect. *We* are not perfect! Nonetheless, even if the people in our lives are trying, they can still be our companions.

"Look again at what faith wants to give you."

Starting with his right index finger, Father Mike counted off the gifts of faith:

"Love of self. Because we realize that God has made us who we are.

"Peace with what we cannot change. Because we realize that whatever cannot be changed has happened for God's good reasons.

"Freedom from fear and pressure. Because we know that everything that is going to happen will also follow God's plan.

"Freedom to love and therefore to live the only life that can bring us happiness. Because we know that love is what life is for—and it doesn't matter whether we are rewarded here.

"Control. Because we can always do what we want most.

"Freedom from the dread of death—or the need to live a life spent distracting ourselves from it. Because we know that death is not the end.

"Freedom from anguish at the death of those we love. Because we know that they are alive with God and that someday we are going to be reunited.

"Freedom to dream joyfully. Because we know that the greatest life we can imagine, and more, is on the way.

"Freedom from longing and envy. Because we know we were made for life with God and nothing here can fill us.

"The ability to enjoy what we already have. Because we do not expect things to be more than they can be."

That made ten.

"All this for seeing the truth that is available to all of us, all the time."

ONCE AGAIN, THE DOCTRINE OF THE FAMILY

"But wait," said Father Mike, "there was one more thing we talked about last time. It was our answer to the question, 'Why, according to God's plan, do some grow so much more than others? And what are we to think when a baby dies and does not grow at all?'"

Mark, who had been present at the first talk, was the first person to put up his hand.

"We are going to be a family."

"Exactly!" said Father Mike. "One idea makes *complete* sense out of all the other basics that explain our lives. And it is something we have spoken out loud all our lives without knowing exactly what we mean ... every time we make the sign of the Cross 'in the name of the Father, and of the Son, and of the Holy Spirit.'"

People looked a little surprised.

"We talked about the idea that God is a family, more than one person as you or I are one person, right?"

At this, many attendees began to nod.

"We saw that this truth is actually obvious in the simple fact that God has made so many things that could never have existed if He had made just one person with whom to share His life, like friendship, romance ... baseball.

"We said that these things could not have been new to God when they first existed here. In other words, the first time two people fell in love, God wasn't watching and saying to Himself, 'What is this all about?'"

This got a laugh.

"No, if something can exist here, it must have existed 'in' God first. And this includes all the many things that can exist only because more than one of us is involved.

"This is what we mean when we say that God is more than one person.

"God made a *family* with whom to share His life. And we are going to share God's life *as* a family, sharing with each other what each one sees in God, just like in a family, the way families are supposed to be!

This way, in the end, all of us will share fully in what our family gets from God."

SOMETHING NEW ABOUT THE DOCTRINE OF THE FAMILY

"Now," said Father Mike, "today I want to expand on the idea of *how* we are going to share God's life as a family."

A newcomer in the front row looked up at Father Mike, seeming more puzzled than inspired.

Father Mike continued. "When we hear about the idea that we are a family, and we are going to share God's life *as* a family, instinctively we get it!

"For sure we get the idea that we are a family—brothers and sisters of the same Father.

"And the idea that we are going to share God's life *as* a family ... well, if we are *together* in heaven, and if you and I are getting something great from God ... well, if we love one another, won't we share what each of us gets from God?"

Father Mike continued. "But how, exactly? This is the question we are tackling today.

"Let's start by talking about how any of us gets *anything* from God in heaven. This is something that we talked about before. We said that once we die and are remade of the same stuff that God is made of, we will be able to see Him.

"And seeing Him face-to-face will teach us more in a moment than we could have learned in a billion years here on earth, where we see God only partly, and learn about Him bit by bit.

"Seeing God face-to-face will, in a moment, make us all we can be. This is how we 'go to heaven.'"

Father Mike continued. "I hope," he said, "that describing heaven in terms of 'seeing God' makes sense. For most of us, sight is the most informative of the senses. Seeing is how we receive from the larger world the information that makes our spirits greater."

"Didn't we just receive this information by hearing?" Jerome said, but only to himself.

"To put it more simply," said Father Mike, "to see is to know. And knowledge gives a greater life.

"But, let us notice: knowledge is something that can be shared. We do it all the time! I hope we're doing it right now!"

This provoked smiles.

Father Mike continued. "And let's look at how we might imagine sharing our sight of God in heaven.

"Let's use the image of God as a statue. There He is in the middle of a room. Many people are gathered around Him; this represents us together in heaven. Now, some of us were very holy on earth, people of great love. We see God well; we are up close. Others among us were not so holy. We see God from further back. But each of us still sees God from his own particular angle. This is a view that no one else can have. If we then share with one another what each of us sees, everyone will know all that might be known about God.

"Now," continued Father Mike, "just like the sharing of knowledge here, sharing what we see in God will take nothing away from anyone but will only make everyone richer. We can picture *this* idea in terms of light. There is a dark room filled with people holding unlit candles. Someone enters with a light. This person proceeds to light the candles of those he meets, and they in turn light the candles of those near them. Soon the room is filled with much light, and everyone will share it. This includes the person who entered with the light. He sees much better than if he had failed to share his light. In heaven, each of us will shine according to our holiness. But the light from each of us will give more light to all so that everybody can see God better.

"Perhaps someone has recognized that I just described what happens at the beginning of the Easter Vigil service."

There were smiles of recognition.

"And just to complete the picture," added Father Mike, "the light we share will further transform and bring out even more in everyone. These fruits will also be shared. And this will bring out even more in everyone ... and so it will go *FOREVER*."

This thought seemed exciting to some, but a little disturbing to Justin, the newcomer in the front row.

"Now," continued Father Mike, "I hope the idea that 'we are going to share God's life as a family and all of us are going to be richer for the holiness of each of us' makes more sense.

"And if this idea makes more sense, we can make sense of many other concepts that we could not wrap our minds around before!

"Now we can understand why God has made us who we are by means of human history, where what *we* have is owed to people of times past who did not have the same advantages that have helped us to know and grow.

"And we can make sense of much that goes on today. After all, if the purpose of history is to make us grow, this means that over time, more and more people will grow—in better and better ways. But this also means that at any one time, there will be many people way behind those who were given by God to lead the way. So those further along need to keep sharing the light of faith to help others advance!

"Knowing this is what helps us make sense of the death of a baby. It is true that the baby didn't grow much, but his or her death affects history; it affects the parents, and their friends, and lots of other people whom the baby did *not* grow up with—all people who will someday be part of our family in heaven. The effects on earth can be very painful—certainly—but in the end, they will lead us to becoming exactly the family God wants with Him in heaven: a family perfectly prepared, according to His plan, and ready to share His life as richly as any family ever could. And as a member of that family who did the job he or she was given to do, the baby will share fully in all that our heavenly family will get from God.

"And, once again, how do we know that all this ... that the doctrine of the family is true?!"

Here Father Mike paused, but not for long.

"We know that the doctrine of the family is true because it makes beautiful sense out of everything else we experience to be true!

"We know because it's *right*—we *do* owe each other for who we are.

"We know because it's *love*—to share all we have with everyone in our family is nothing less than what love will want to do.

"And we know the doctrine of the family is true because we were made for sharing. We were made for each other—our lives are nothing unless we share them."

WHY WE NEED TO BE A FAMILY OF FAITH ON EARTH

"We were made for each other," repeated Father Mike. "This is our experience all the time. It is our experience in terms of faith. You know that when the church is full, people feel more certain. And, unfortunately, churches that are often empty almost always get emptier.

"You know that you feel more confident when people agree with you. And when they don't, they provoke you to doubt—at least a little.

"Isn't it also human experience that when we work together, we get more done?

"Isn't it obvious that if we are united, we will be much more effective at moving the world in the direction God wants it to go?!

"Obviously, then, because we are going to share God's life as a family, we are 'in this together' here.

"That's why God wants us to be a family of faith here on earth.

"But, as we discussed at our first talk ... although we talked about it quickly ... if God wanted us to be a family, He had to send someone to call us to be a family. A family in faith cannot come together by some grand coincidence of agreement. And this is where Jesus comes into the picture.

ENTER JESUS

"Let us think this through together.

"A Church cannot exist because a bunch of people all happen to come up with the same ideas and decide to form a group. Someone has to determine what exactly is the formula that lets the participants believe together.

"Oh sure," interjected Father Mike, quickly, "each participant will understand everything a little bit differently. That's actually everyone's job— to become someone who will see God in a special way and have this to share with everyone else. But our formulas can still allow us to agree about certain essential ideas, so we will feel supported by one another's faith.

"And we are not going to get to such formulas by chance or through public opinion.

"Also, if we are going to get together to share our faith, someone has to decide where, and when, and what we will do.

"No," continued Father Mike, "if we are going to help the world to become what God wants it to be, we will need to work together, and this presumes leadership.

"So, who will be our leader?"

Now Father Mike paused a bit too long.

"How about you?" asked Henry. This, of course, got a good laugh.

"Oh, you think the idea is funny?" answered Father Mike. And this got another laugh.

Father Mike picked up where he left off. "So who will be our leader?

"Whom *should* we listen to, thinking that this is what God wants us to do? Whom should we listen to, thinking that this is what God wants us to do *even though*, in this world, where everyone is made to see things differently, we will not always agree?

"Who, on his own authority, has the right to speak to you in the name of God?

"Should it be the holiest person? Who, precisely, is that?" No comments, but a few more laughs.

Father Mike continued. "And what happens when the holy person turns out not to be so holy ... or not so smart?

"Perhaps we should reward the most convincing person. But what if he does not convince absolutely everyone? And what happens tomorrow when an even more convincing person appears? Then when this more convincing person dies?"

People knew that these were not questions expecting an answer.

Father Mike continued. "No, surely it is clear, if God wanted us to be a family in faith, He had to send someone to start this family.

"How does He do this? How does He do it in a way that does *NOT* overwhelm us, so that we still need to get to faith by our own growing?

"God's way was to have this person appear according to His plan, to have this person call people together in the name of His truth, and then to do something to identify this person as the one He has sent.

"How do we know that this was Jesus? Put simply, we get to know him."

GETTING TO KNOW JESUS

"For the first Christians," said Father Mike, "it was, in one way, easy.

"They knew Jesus personally in the flesh; they witnessed his life and death; and then some of them were given an experience of him in glory. We call this the Resurrection. This is what God did to identify Jesus, and no one else, as the one He had sent to start His family.

"Just to be clear," said Father Mike, "when we are talking about the Resurrection, we are not—not right now, not in tonight's talk—trying to be too specific. All we are saying is that, at some time after Jesus died, God gave the apostles a glimpse of Jesus in glory, in the spiritual body we talked about last time. The bottom line is this: God did something unmistakable to let the apostles know that Jesus was alive, and that Jesus had taught the truth.

"We who came after them," continued Father Mike, "get to know Jesus through the story of his life—we call this the Gospel—and then we, too, experience his Resurrection."

Joy, not a newcomer, put up her hand. "I'm not sure I can say that I ever experienced the Resurrection," she said.

"I know," responded Father Mike, "that most people who say 'I believe in the Resurrection' *don't* say that they *experience* it. But if their faith is deep, this is, in fact, what is happening.

"Without necessarily being able to explain their thinking, here's what happens: they experience directly the truth of the faith they got from Jesus and his Church.

"This includes the truth that 'we were made to be a family.'

"They see that we cannot be a family unless *God* has called us to be one.

24

"They see that this means God had to send some-one to speak for Him, and to do something unique to identify this person as the one He has sent.

"They experience this in the person of Jesus, in the story of his death and Resurrection.

"And then, in prayer, they experience Jesus alive, listening to them."

Joy looked intrigued by this answer.

Father Mike continued. "Besides this," he said, "looking at the world, we ask: Who else can it be? Who has records from multiple sources that date within a generation from the time of such miraculous events? Whose following got its start from the testimony of people whose word did not glorify *themselves* but rather told of their cowardice and scattering—only to be called back together *without their leader present* and inspired to go on, face persecution and eventu-ally death, and do such a tremendous job of planting the faith that, more than any other, has transformed the world?"

Father Mike was not done. "And besides all this ...

"If someone gives up his life *and lives*, don't you see the reality that there *is* a heaven?

"If someone gives up his life and gets to glory, don't you see the glory in love?

"If someone gives his life up because God the Father doesn't give him a better option not to, *and it works out*, don't you see the wisdom of God's plan?

"See? The Resurrection not only confirmed that Jesus taught the truth; it confirmed the truth that Jesus taught. Don't you see the hand of God in this?!"

Some people nodded. Others still looked unconvinced.

ENTER THE CHURCH

"Now," said Father Mike, "let's make sure that we understand the implications of what we're saying.

"The whole idea of Jesus and the Resurrection comes from the fact—which we can verify for ourselves at any time—that we are called to be a family in faith.

"This means that someone has to keep us together and guide us going forward—today.

"Who would this be? In other words, once Jesus returned to the Father, where did His authority go?"

People nodded, following him.

"Let's start with the facts," said Father Mike. "Jesus in glory was *not* experienced by everyone he ever talked to, or even all his followers. Rather, he was experienced by people who were chosen and prepared for this experience, who from the beginning were recognized as leaders. These were the apostles. *Their* leader, the leader that Jesus named to take over after him, was Saint Peter. This was how the Church started.

"Thereafter, as the Church began to grow, and time went on, the apostles realized that they were going to have to appoint new leaders to carry on. They invented the ceremony of the laying on of hands—what we now call 'ordination'—for this purpose. From this, the structure of the Church developed. Through ordination, then, the Church is based on an actual *physical* connection to Jesus. Think of a game of tag—each new apostle is 'it.'"

"Now," continued Father Mike, "if we understand that the purpose of all this is to keep us ONE, where else but in our Church is this idea still working? Where else but in our Church, which has conserved the position of Saint Peter in the person of the pope, is there any claim to the kind of authority that a truly united, worldwide Church would need?

"Now, for those of you who know a little about Church history and maybe are not happy about everything the Church has ever done—or even some of the things going on today—please remember this: We are here for the purpose of growing, not just as individuals but as a family. And growing out of what? Growing out of ignorance and selfishness. That's true for the Church, too. This means that at any given time we will be at least a little ... not smart, and sinful. It means we will always have a long way to go. But this has to be OK. This is what we're here for!

"And growing is what has been happening. Slowly but surely, most of the time, we have been going forward, understanding God better, becoming a holier people. And this will keep happening if we keep trying. It has to. If God's plan brought about Jesus to start the Church, then surely this same plan is going to make sure that the Church, by means of many struggles, goes forward to where it must go.

"The Church was not ordained by God in order to fail. It cannot fail. It will go forward perfecting our knowledge of God, making humanity holier, and making us one.

"None of this is easy. Growing is hard. To go forward, we eventually have to leave some things behind. But we can do it. We can grasp deeper ideas than we started with. We can let go of what we no longer need. We can do what we are here for and grow.

"Does anyone need to use the bathroom?"

A number of people got up and formed lines at opposite ends of the church hall.

After a short break, Father Mike continued.

"Before we go on, I would like to answer a question that someone asked me during the break. The question was: Shouldn't Church members get to vote for their leaders?"

Some audience members nodded fiercely at the suggestion. Others rolled their eyes.

"Let me begin," said Father Mike, "by pointing out that it was *almost never thus*. On instinct, I suppose, the first Church leaders understood that the people they were bringing into the Church were just starting out on their Christian journeys. They didn't know as much about the faith as those they learned it from. And when the first Church leaders did *well* and brought in lots and lots of new members, there was no way this new majority was going to be able to vote on *truth!*"

It started to sound as though Father Mike was giving a political speech. In this vein, he continued. "Jesus didn't put his teachings up for a vote. And as far as we know, he didn't even consult anyone when he picked people to help him and take over after him. Instead, he picked people whom *he* knew understood his teachings best.

"And it's fair to presume, most of the time in this imperfect world, these people who understood best would be in the best position to know whom *they* should choose to help and follow after them. This is our system. It is not perfect, but it is still the best way to provide leadership for a family that is based on TRUTH."

More slowly and with a softer voice, Father Mike continued.

"Now it is also true that as we as a people keep on growing, more and more people are increasingly capable of contributing worthwhile points of view. Certainly we see this in our communities, and we see it in the Church. The pastor isn't the only one who knows things, nor the only one with good ideas."

This brought about smiles—probably not for the best of reasons.

"This, of course, is the way it should be. That everyone has something special to offer is the purpose of life here and the way that things will be in heaven.

"And so the Church must find ways to let this happen. And, frankly, it *is* happening. We have words for it like 'consultation' and 'constitutionality' ..."

Father Mike read the confusion on people's faces and added quickly, "that second word means that you have rights."

People smiled—this time for a good reason. Father Mike picked up where he left off. "Consultation, constitutionality, and subsidiarity ..."

More puzzled faces.

"Subsidarity means that, to the extent you can get away with it and still have unity, decisions should be made at the level closest to the people who will have to live out the decisions."

Father Mike added, "It's the reason your pastor doesn't try to tell you what toothpaste to use."

This got a laugh.

"At this point," said Father Mike, "I would like us to move on to the next topic we should talk about. We have covered the beauty and rightness of Jesus giving up his life. Let's talk a little more about *how* Jesus gave up his life. Let's talk about the Cross."

THE CROSS

"Let's look at what actually happened."

"Jesus is teaching a new and even deeper idea of God than he had learned about through his Jewish faith. He is inspiring people, making the religious and political leaders of the time envious. They plot to have him killed. He is warned and has to decide whether to stay or to run. He decides that if he is to represent for real the faith he is teaching, he must stay. He ends up being crucified.

"This awful thing happened according to God's plan. It must have been meant to tell us a lot.

"Now I know," said Father Mike, "that the Cross means much more than I can say in just a few sentences. But we can still talk about some of the more powerful aspects.

"The first we have *already* seen," continued Father Mike. "If someone gives up his life *and lives*, don't you see heaven? If someone gives up his life and gets to glory, don't you see the glory in love? If someone gives his life up because God the Father doesn't give him a better option not to, *and it works out*, don't you see the wisdom of God's plan?"

The answers, of course, were obvious. Father Mike continued.

"Besides this, since Jesus was sent to represent God the Father ... well, he represents Him across the board!

"In other words, he represents what the Father thinks and he represents how the Father feels.

"So I think it's safe to assume that he looked at people—God's other children—with love. That includes the Gentiles, the pagans—most of our ancestors, in other words!

"And he had enough love for them that he was willing to risk his life by not running. Then, when he could still have escaped by recanting his teachings, he didn't; he was willing to give up his life."

Father Mike's tone of voice now became softer, more tender.

"To give up one's life is the most one can do in the name of love.

"It can come only from the greatest love that one can have.

"This is what the Father feels when He looks at us, the children He has made so He can love us with the greatest love that He can have.

"Please ... remember ... we've seen this already. God does nothing halfway; if He loves us, He loves us with all His heart. And He can love us with His whole heart only because He has put His whole life into making each of us, every detail of His plan for our lives. We've seen this already. And this is one of the things the Cross is trying to say!"

Here there was a slight pause.

"But there's more. It's fairly obvious that Jesus *suffered* on the Cross, suffered a lot.

"It's also easy to understand that his Father suffered with him, as parents do.

"But in the case of the Father ... He does not look upon the suffering of his Son and *imagine* how bad it is. He knows precisely how bad it is. But for this to be true ... to know *precisely* how something feels ... He has to feel it, too, as though it were Him.

"And this is true, not just when He looked at what was happening to Jesus; it is also true when He looks at what is happening to all of us, His children, all the time. This is another meaning of the Cross—that God suffers with us in everything we go through."

People sat up in their chairs with particular interest. Father Mike was well aware how difficult it is to speak about suffering. Brows furrowed and people looked serious.

"God," he said, "knows that life can be hard. He also knows that life is worth it—that by going through hard things, sometimes very hard things, there is so much more that He can give us. But He knows these things *are* hard; and to make it as bearable for us as He can, He bears them with us. This is another meaning of the Cross!"

Some people nodded. Others seemed more confused than ever. So Father Mike continued, eager to bring this point home.

"There's one more thing," said Father Mike. "Representing the Father, Jesus gave up his life. Now, it would not be possible to say that the Father also 'died.' It is possible, however, to say that the Father gave up His life in the sense that He gave *of* it."

Another slight pause.

"Let us think this through together.

"God is the source of all that is or can be.

"Nothing exists apart from God and nothing can exist if He does not sustain it.

"And how does He do that? He sustains things by His will, His power, His love. And where His will is, He is!

"Don't you see? We are made not just *by* God but *of* Him, of His love. To give us life, He has 'diverted,' or maybe we should say 'dedicated,' some of what He *is* to give us life.

"And what should this mean to us, apart from showing us that God's love for us is even greater than we'd thought?

"It tells us that God is as close to us as our own skin. We are that valuable! And, of course, God knows what we are going through. Of course, we are absolutely safe in His hands.

"See all the things that God wanted to show us on the Cross?!"

Again Father Mike counted off with his fingers.

"The truth of our basic faith.

"That He could not love us more.

"That He suffers with us everything we go through.

"And that we are made of His love.

"And see what else God has done? So that we could see the sacrifice of the Cross *live and in color*, all through the centuries and all around the world, He convened the Last Supper."

THE MASS

By now people had figured out that they were hearing something a little different. Nick wasn't sure he liked it.

Father Mike continued.

"Jesus knows that his enemies are coming to get him. He has decided not to run. He needs to do something so that his mission can go on. He has to ... the word is 'commission' ... his main followers to carry on. He needs some sort of action that will do this. And he wants to give them something they will not lose.

"Blessing bread and wine, and giving it to people to eat and drink, does this.

"But," there was now a bit of urgency in Father Mike's voice, "please understand, as far as Jesus is concerned, he is not just giving his followers a job—*he is giving them himself.*

"A person with a mission does not distinguish between himself and his mission."

Some people nodded.

"Jesus was giving himself to his followers," he said, "but God the Father planned the Last Supper to do even more.

"Clearly, the Last Supper took place according to God's plan," said Father Mike, "and certainly God knew that by the very nature of it—as Jesus' last supper—it was going to be repeated by Jesus' followers when they got together to share a meal. Jesus had *told* them to do this, in memory of him.

"Once they started doing this, they began to see more and more in it.

"Over time, this is where our beautiful doctrine of the Mass came from.

"Today, to keep it simple:

"One," said Father Mike. "Mass gives us a repeatable way to see that moment when, with a decision he could not take back, Jesus truly gave up his life.

"A repeatable way," repeated Father Mike, "since it's pretty obvious that we can't repeat the Crucifixion.

"Two. The blessing of the bread and wine *makes* something that, obviously and naturally, represents all the messages of the Cross.

"This is something we can *see* ... not just hear about, something we can *receive personally*, so each of us knows that 'God is talking to *me*, too, and just as much to me as to anyone else' ... after all, no one gets *more* Communion than others.

"And this is something we can even *eat* ... and then we can never lose it, since it has become part of us. This is just like the love of God that we can never lose, because our whole lives take place in His plan!

"And three. Mass gives a sacred meal that makes us not just a 'congregation' but a *family* in faith—a *family* because sharing supper is what makes families ... families!"

"And in case you've always wanted to know how Communion is the Body of Christ ..."

Nick was all ears.

"Think of it this way," said Father Mike. "What *was* the body of Christ? In other words, what was the Body of Christ we would want to receive?

"The Body of Christ we would want to receive was the Body of Christ on the Cross, which was a message. It was, as we saw, God's way of saying 'I could not love you more.'

"But God wanted to give His people a sign of His love that could be seen by everyone everywhere, over and over again. He therefore inspired the Last Supper that was sure to become our Mass.

"And do notice," added Father Mike, "that the Mass was well designed to accomplish its purpose.

"After all, Jesus may have died on the Cross, but he really gave up his life the night before, at the Last Supper, when, in the blessing of the bread and wine, he revealed his decision not to run away, knowing that his enemies were coming to arrest and ultimately kill him.

"This was the moment at which Jesus gave up his life, and the Mass presents it as perfectly as it can be presented. We have all that we could possibly bring together. We have the table, the bread, and the wine. We have a person ordained to represent Jesus every day in every way, who uses the very same words Jesus used at the Last Supper. And the people are real disciples.

"We have everything that was there at the first Last Supper. We are going to see that moment when Jesus gave up his life—God's way of showing that He could not love us more, that He has put all that He could into our making. In the process—and here Mass is even more effective than the Cross—we see a sign that we can also receive and even eat."

"I know all of this is a lot," said Father Mike. "But I have one more thing for us tonight.

"Not only the Cross and the Last Supper were planned by God to inspire us. No, everything about the life of Jesus was planned by God for our benefit. Let's take a quick look at the life of Jesus."

There was some resettling in chairs.

THE LIFE OF JESUS

"Let's start with the Christmas story," said Father Mike, "which says that Jesus was born in a manger.

"Does anybody happen to know some French?"

This question caught people by surprise but three or four put up their hands.

"Manger," repeated Father Mike. "Please pronounce this word as though it were French."

A couple of people were able to do it.

"And what does this word mean?" asked Father Mike.

And someone said out loud, "Eat." And everybody got the point!

"Jesus was born in a place where animals eat." Father Mike wanted to make sure that everybody got the point.

"Jesus was born poor.

"Jesus was born poor, and this was just the beginning of an awful life in which he was going to suffer some version of just about every hard thing that can happen to anyone.

"Jesus was born poor—but this didn't stop him.

"He lost his human father early in his life—but this didn't stop him. And this is an especially important message for those many, many young people *not* being raised by a father in the house, who often think badly about themselves for this reason.

"Jesus spent most of the rest of his life as an anonymous worker taking care of his mother.

"This is an especially important example for today," said Father Mike, "when fame is glorified, and those who are not famous, who 'just' work, think they are unimportant. In part, Jesus' life was meant to glorify work, honest work, and responsibly taking care of the people who need you."

This point got Mark's attention.

"When, finally, Jesus came to his mission, people did not understand him. Jesus talked about the 'kingdom of God.' The people of his time thought he was talking about a revolution against the Romans—and this is what they wanted, as if this would have solved all their problems. Jesus was offering so much more—survive death, see God, so much more—but they were crazy for so much less. This certainly is the experience of many people who discover the wonder of a life of faith and want to share it with others—and find that others care only about cars, television, or going to parties.

"When Jesus finally started getting through to people, he ran into opposition. Mostly because they were envious of the attention he was getting, the religious establishment of the time, the Pharisees, were against him at every turn. This is certainly the experience of many who are trying to do good and run into opposition for no good reason—even in the Church!

"Jesus' enemies got one of his followers—and, presumably, one of his *friends*, Judas—to set him up to be arrested. This happened so that if *you* are betrayed by someone you have loved ... you will understand that *God understands*. You will realize that betrayal is the fault of the betrayer. This is especially important because, in their hearts, most people who have been betrayed blame themselves—if only I had been better, more beautiful, more talented.... Well, not in Jesus' case, and not in yours either."

Gloria was seemingly touched by this.

Father Mike continued. "When Jesus was arrested the rest of his friends abandoned him. Enough said.

"The person he had chosen as his successor, Peter, denied that he knew him. This was so that if people pretend not to know *you*, because it is not 'cool' in the eyes of some to know you, you know who you are in the eyes of God.

"Jesus suffered emotionally in the garden where he was waiting for the tortures he knew were coming.

"He was tortured physically—in case you have to bear terrible physical pain.

"He was condemned unjustly, because people lied about him."

Henry bent forward, looking down at the floor.

"He was abused by people he was trying to help. He was mocked and humiliated, and naked on the Cross.

"He died alone, a complete and total failure in the eyes of the world.

"This was the life of Jesus," said Father Mike.

"And why was Jesus asked to live such a life? So that if we are betrayed, abandoned, or condemned unjustly, we will not feel that we are worthless. So that we will know that God understands anything we ever suffer. So that we will know that, like Jesus, we can conquer any adversity if only by accepting it."

Seeing that his audience looked a little weary after this march through the life of Christ, Father Mike reassured them.

"I'm almost done."

PRESENTATION OF THE PRACTICAL CREEDS

"Before we finish tonight, I'd like you to notice that, broadly speaking, I have added three new ideas to the four we talked about last time.

"Last time we talked about the four ideas— heaven, love, God's plan, and the fact that we were made to be a family—that explain life and give us the gifts of faith.

"Today we have talked about three ideas that give the basic ideas flesh and help us to see them, be inspired by them, and celebrate them.

"If we put them all together, we get what I would offer to you as 'A Practical Creed.' This creed is practical in the sense that it explains Christianity in such a way as to have the most impact on the human spirit with the fewest words. Let's go through it ..."

For the first time, Father Mike read aloud:

A PRACTICAL CREED

God made us for life in heaven.

The way to heaven is a life of faith and love.

God guides us according to His plan for everything He sends into our lives.

We are going to share heaven as a family where all of us are going to be richer for the holiness of each of us.

Jesus was sent to teach the truth, to found the Church, and to accept the Cross on which he taught and showed us love.

The Eucharist is the meal we share to be God's family, and it is also God's way to show us again and again the love He showed us first on the Cross.

The rest of the life of Jesus was planned to show us that faith can conquer any adversity.

"I really like 'A Practical Creed,'" said Father Mike. "It's clear and simple. It's meaningful—every article gives us so much just for understanding it. And best of all, properly explained, who can't see it?!

"Don't you see? Here is the formula for the future union of all believers! The 'Practical Creed' is a great guide for sharing faith with just about anyone!

"Okay," said Father Mike, with a small change of tone indicating that he was slightly embarrassed. "I know I said I was almost done, but as long as we are talking about 'A Practical Creed,' I'd like to share with you two more that are related to it.

"The first," announced Father Mike, "is called 'Practically, a Creed.'"

Again reading:

My dreams are sure to come true in heaven.

Even if I got what I want now, soon I would be preoccupied with something else.

Someday I am going to be so very happy I went through this.

If I've done all I can, I can give it back to God.

It doesn't matter what people think.

Since faith is its own reward, no one gets away with anything.

In the end, everything is going to be as it should be.

"That one is meant to help us get through, day to day. I've got one more, intended to keep our eyes on the prize. Let's just call it 'PC III.'

No one really dies.

Our every effort of love will make all of us richer forever.

We will be thrilled with the results of everything we went through.

In heaven, no one will be beneath or above me.

The Cross was God's way of saying "I could not love you more."

Communion presents the love behind the Cross equally to each of us.

Whatever we go through, Jesus went through it before us, and went that way to glory.

"Okay, we're done; I really mean it this time." People laughed.

"To finish up, I would like to suggest a way you can use what we have talked about these last two meetings ... to get the most out of faith, to keep it in front of you, and to keep it growing. Just keep 'The Four Pillars.'

"And before I go through them, I would like you to know that I have fliers to remind you of all these things I am reading to you tonight.

"Here they are."

THE FOUR PILLARS

1. Post "A Practical Creed" where you will often see it. Read it whenever you have the chance.

2. Say the "Our Father" every day, and mean it. Be aware that when you say, "Thy kingdom come," you are acknowledging that nothing is more important than heaven, and when you say, "Thy will be done," you are acknowledging that God's plan for you always knows best.

3. Treat others as you want them to treat you. (In moments of conflict, strive to see the situation from the other person's point of view.)

4. Come to church. Be as faithful to God as you want God to be faithful to you.

Father Mike looked up.

"Let's go over it," he said.

"Number 1 is pretty straightforward. Perhaps it doesn't seem like a very big deal, but the way human nature works, there is a huge amount to be gained by repetition. By repetition, we make things part of us.

"In the case of 'A Practical Creed,' over the course of time—just a couple of months, probably—you will instinctively see everything in the light of faith. And everything will look better.

"For Number 2, the key is 'mean it.' If we have thought things through and really *mean it* when we say, in effect, 'Nothing is more important than heaven,' then what we do and don't have on earth just doesn't matter. If we really mean it when we say 'Thy will be done,' of course we get peace!

"Number 3, the Golden Rule, helps us answer the question: If in fact we are here to grow in love, what must we actually do? And the part about striving to see things from another person's point of view ... it's the main way we identify *chances* to treat others the way we want them to treat us. And if we are *inspired* by moments of conflict ... well, let's face it; we'll get chances all day long!"

People laughed. Some looked at each other.

"Number 4 is a big one to me. I speak often about the gifts of faith, and I notice that everybody wants them. They want them, but they don't do anything to show themselves that they really believe. Remember, talk is cheap. If you truly believe that God really does want us to be a family in faith, and that by practicing your faith you are sure to make it grow, and that by coming to church you are helping everyone else to grow in a richer life for all forever—you will come to church. It's an hour, once a week!"

People laughed, some looking sheepish. "And feel free to call me with any questions that might come up for you.

"Thank you for listening."

Father Mike now got a generous applause. In the days ahead he would get several calls as well—Justin was going to call because of what he heard. Jerome, Nick, and Margaret were going to call because of what they did not hear. Others were going to call because they were in pain. ■

■

JUSTIN
(WANTS TO KNOW
IF WE BELIEVE IN HELL)

Justin arrived for his appointment on time, introduced himself, and went straight to the heart of the matter: "I came to your talks, Father, and I liked them; but I got the idea that you are saying that no matter what you do, you're going to heaven. Is this right?"

"Well, Justin," replied Father Mike, "I guess the short answer is yes, but please don't get the idea that it doesn't matter what you do with your life."

"How does it matter?"

"Remember, Justin, we are here for a reason. God is giving us a chance to participate in our own creation—to become our own persons. We do this by growing, by growing in the faith and love that makes us more like Him so that we can share His life more richly. The more we grow, the richer our lives will be forever."

"But didn't you also say that everybody is going to share 'fully' in heaven? I think you said that several times."

Father Mike smiled. "I probably did. But that doesn't mean it doesn't matter what we do. One of the most important things I wanted you to get from my talks is the idea that we were made to be a family, and we are going to share God's life *as* a family.

"This means that the more you grow, and help others to do the same, the richer the life will be that we are going to share—and this means you, too!"

Father Mike went on. "This idea, that we are going to share God's life as a family, is hugely important. It makes sense out of everything else that we believe. Without it ... how do we explain the goodness of God's plan when a baby dies who never got a chance to grow?

"How do we explain the goodness of God's plan when we look at the lives of so many people in this world who were born into faithless families, or other bad situations, or who were born in places far from a chance to hear about faith and get it?

"The idea of the family makes sense of history. After all, the way God made us, what you and I have, is due to progress, and the lives and deaths of countless people of the past who had no chance to hear or understand the things we are talking about *right now*. But because of them, we get this chance. Am I talking too fast?"

"It's okay."

"Okay, then, don't you see that we owe those people—and that we should share with them what we are going to get from the special way that we will see and understand God?"

"Maybe them," said Justin, "and maybe babies who had no chance, but what about those people out there, those people who are really bad. Do they deserve a 'share,' too?"

"I can see how it doesn't look right, Justin, at first. But I also know that it is dangerous when we start deciding who are the good people and who are the bad. It's just not that simple. What *is* simple is that people do the best they can with what they are given. And some people were given *very little* ... in fact, they were given a really bad set of experiences, and the best they could do was not too good."

"What about all those people," asked Justin, "who were given little and did *great*, and those who were given everything and became monsters?"

"Please understand, Justin, when we talk about things that people were 'given,' we are not just talking about material things or other worldly advantages. We are also talking about good example. We are talking about discipline, the discipline that spares children from becoming monsters. We are talking about *not* being spoiled by your parents who have money. We are talking about being fortunate enough to be influenced by *good* friends, fortunate enough to be ready inside when life sends the first hard things we have to go through. No, often times people who look poor were really given more than people who look rich.

"I would also like to mention," added Father Mike, "that to look at people with compassion because 'they do the best they can with what they have been given,' is the supremely right reason to have compassion when you look in the mirror.

"Of course, your job, and mine, is to keep learning, keep thinking, and keep striving to do better. And I hope that hearing this is another of the good things that you've been given!"

Justin frowned. "So it's all about what you've been given. What about free will?"

"Well, Justin," said Father Mike, "let's go over what we said about free will. We said that free will is *not* about some power to make choices completely apart from everything we have experienced and learned. It is not some power to make choices that surprise even God. Free will means that our choices come from *us*; they reflect us, the people we are inside. And because these choices affect us, they change us, and in this way we are intimately involved in translating our experiences into the people we are. This is how we participate in our own creation. The fact that this process originates in God—and was planned by

Him to create a family perfectly prepared to share His life—was just smart!"

Justin persevered. "How do some of these monsters belong in a family perfectly prepared to share God's life?"

"I guess it doesn't look like it! But let's think about some of the things we have talked about lately.

"We have figured out that we are here to participate in our creation *as the family* that we are going to be in heaven. The purpose of life is for *us* to help God make *us*.

"And," added Father Mike, "if our participation is such a big deal, then isn't it true that the more we contribute the better?"

Justin nodded, clearly still unsure about what he was agreeing to.

Father Mike continued. "This means that the human race had to start out *far* from what we might grow into. That's why in the beginning we were just *barely* more than animals.

"And so that *more* people could contribute, God is making us by a process that, to us, looks *slow*—by means of history, by means of centuries of struggle.

"This means that, as time goes by, more and more people will do better and better. It also means that, at any given time, a bunch of people will be behind. And some people will be far behind."

Justin smiled thinly. "This entitles them to a good place in heaven?"

"It is God, Justin, who gives the jobs. Some people got the job of making the human conquest of evil the really great thing that it will be."

"I don't get what you mean there."

Father Mike responded, "If what our family is going to accomplish can be called 'great,'" he said, "we need to overcome some things that are really terrible. After all," explained Father Mike, "if we start out as almost perfect people who do no more than make our lives a little better, our spirits are not really the product of anything great that *we* have done. But if we start out in ignorance and selfishness, and all sorts of weakness and capacity for craziness and cruelty, and overcome all that ... then we have done something great. And that's been the case all throughout history.

"But for this to happen ... somebody has to embody the problems that we are called overcome.

"Actually," Father Mike interrupted himself to clarify, "it is still a mistake to talk about who is the 'problem' and who is the 'solution'—just as it was wrong to talk about who is 'good' and who is 'bad.' In truth, all of us have some good in us even if it's not always near the surface, and all of us are *far* from good compared to what we are going to be in heaven."

"So there's no hell?"

"Did you want there to be hell?"

"It's not about what *I* want."

"Perhaps not, Justin, but do you feel you could be 'perfectly' happy in heaven knowing that people, maybe even people you love, are writhing in agony—and will be forever?!"

"I admit it doesn't sound right," replied Justin, "but I was taught that there's a hell."

"I know, Justin," said Father Mike, "but we have been talking about the idea that life here is about our human family growing up. Well, growing up means growing up into deeper and deeper ideas, including a deeper idea of God. In times past, people thought of God as a judge who was quick to condemn them. This is how religion 'inspired' people to be good.

"But we have grown into a deeper idea of God and His love, and the reason for life, and so forth. Now we really *can't* imagine a God who would give us life, give us rules, and then send us to suffer forever because we didn't satisfy His rules. And remember, nobody asks to be born!

"Now we understand that hell was the only way that people of times past could make sense of the idea that what we do makes an eternal difference.

"Today, with the doctrine of the family, we have a much better way to make sense of this idea—one that is completely consistent with the deepest idea of God and His love that we can conceive. And certainly God cannot love *less* than we can conceive!

"Hell was once the best way humans could make sense of what we were given. Now we have a better way to explain to people that what they do with their lives makes an eternal difference."

"Same thing with purgatory?"

"The part about the fire, yes. But just as with hell, we still see truth in the doctrine of purgatory. It also was trying to make the point that what we do with our lives matters after we die.

"And there is another truth in the doctrine of purgatory."

"What?"

"In order to see God we will need to be changed. Isn't that true?"

"I guess."

"Of course it's true. God is here right now, and we can't see Him. No, to be able to see Him we will have to be changed."

Justin nodded.

Father Mike continued. "And obviously this change depends on what we give God to start with. Some will have to be changed more than others, won't they? But it doesn't hurt, and it doesn't take time. Again, in the past, the idea that it was time in fire was the only way people could make sense of the idea that every little thing you do matters!"

"But if God's plan is for us to be the best family in heaven, how does every little thing matter?"

"God's plan *is* for us to be the family best prepared to share His life; this is true. The human family will do the job it was meant to do; and it will become the best it could possibly be. But how good is our best? How good is humanity's best? Right now, we don't know. But we do know that our decisions will affect what happens. We know that our purpose is to do what we believe will bring about the best. You and I are in a position to make humanity's best even better—or not.

"But," said Father Mike with a little burst of passion, "we don't have to live with the awful burden of thinking that we can mess up God's plan! In the end, *we are going* to become the family that we were meant to be.

"And, isn't it nice to know that you won't have to face the fire, Justin? Is it *really* more comforting to think that other people will have to face worse?!"

Justin had to think about this for a second. Then he said, "But I'm still having a hard time thinking about certain people being really happy in heaven."

"If you are thinking about certain people who have what look like sinful lives, Justin, please don't think that they are getting away with anything. People who are sin*ful* are also faith*less*.

"People of faith have peace, purpose, and joy that others can't even imagine. People of faith can face death. People of faith are more alive."

"Other people can act happy, but they are really empty.

"Speaking for myself," continued Father Mike, "I never think that people whose lives contradict everything I care about have anything over me! I think *I'm* the one with the better life. I think I got a better job in the working out of God's plan than many other people. We might even say that 'justice' is really on *their* side ... they're the ones who had to live and die without peace or joy.

"But what's really going on is this: To become the family perfectly prepared to share God's life, God needs every person to play a specific part in His plan. They do it; and that's why they belong at the table. And, by the way, in a family, that's the way we want it, isn't it?"

"What do you mean?"

"I mean that in your family you share everything equally, and you are happy to do so—I hope! Well, once we get to heaven, we can see one another as God sees us now.

"Once we are all transformed, and we are all much 'better' than anyone was here, and much better at being sorry for the bad things that we did and much better at being understanding and forgiving ...

"We will recognize each other as family. We will see the beauty that God put into people who looked 'bad' to us here, and we will be thrilled with what they have become and what they will have to share with us!"

"This is a lot to think about," said Justin.

"It is, but I am going to ask you to think about even more."

"What's that?"

"If you came to my talks, you may remember that I said everyone has a reason to be thrilled to be who he or she is—because God has put all He has into that person's making and no less than He has put into the making of anyone else."

"I remember that."

"Then you may also remember that I pointed out that if we *know* that we are no less than anyone else, we have no need to feel that we are more."

"This is a lot to think about," said Justin again.

"It is, Justin," said Father Mike, "but I am going to ask you to think about one more thing."

"Okay," said Justin, giving evidence that he was now a little tired.

"From the beginning, we have talked about the idea that we can make sense of life here, before heaven, with the idea that we are here to be involved in our own creation; and this we do by growing."

"I got that," said Justin.

"But," continued Father Mike, "all of us are called to grow all our lives. And those who have grown a lot, and love goodness, are still able to grow more. In fact, they need to be able to take some giant steps forward if their own struggle to grow is to remain meaningful until it's over."

Justin stayed quiet.

Father Mike continued. "And such people have an opportunity to take a giant step forward if they are able to reach for the greatest compassion they might imagine.

"This is not easy," he added, "but it is not supposed to be.

"It's not easy," repeated Father Mike, "but it's possible once we realize that we often judge things based on a primal instinct to strike back at those who in any way menace us.

"If we can get past this, we should be able to see that life is about growing, the more the better. And if 'the more the better,' we don't need eternal punishments that contradict the boundless love of God in order to insist that 'right' really matters.

"Instead, we have every reason to strive with all our strength, and every reason to live in complete peace, at the same time."

"I'm going to need to think about these things," said Justin. "Maybe read about them. Do you have anything that might help?"

Father Mike was ready with the guide to spiritual reading he gave to almost everyone who came to see him. Atypically, he also gave Justin something he called a guide to "theological" reading.[1] "Please come back," he said, "and let me know about how your thinking is going. There really is an awful lot to be gained."

"I'll let you know," said Justin. "I don't plan to let this go." ■

---

1. You can easily obtain a copy of either for yourself; see the epilogue.

■

JEROME
(WANTS TO KNOW IF WE BELIEVE IN THE BIBLE)

Jerome knew precisely where he was going to begin. He was respectful but edgy when he pointed out to Father Mike, "you never once mentioned hell."

"That's true, Jerome," replied Father Mike. "I guess I was hoping that everyone would recognize that we were talking about a bigger and more beautiful idea of God than maybe they had heard of before, and they would realize that the love of this God has forgiveness for everyone and a place for everyone in the family we are going to be."

"So, there is no hell?"

"If, when we talk about there being 'hell to pay,' we mean that our sins can make heaven poorer, then yes. If we are talking about a place where people will burn in agony forever, then no."

"The Bible says there is a hell."

"That's true, but we do need to remember that the books and letters in the Bible were written a long

63

time ago, to share faith with people who were much simpler than most people today. And back then, the only way people could understand that what we do makes an eternal difference was to think that if they *don't* do it, there will be hell to pay."

"So, there is no hell?"

"Again, if we are talking about a place where people will burn in agony forever, then no."

"And no devil? Don't you believe in the devil?"

"Doesn't it sound funny to say 'I believe *in* the devil'? I know, Jerome, that the scriptures speak in many places about the devil, and demonic possession, and stuff like that, but again, the scriptures were written a long time ago to make sense of things to people who were much simpler than most people today."

Father Mike continued. "When it comes to the devil, we are actually talking about several different ideas at once. First of all, and probably most important, the idea of the devil and demonic possession was the only way the ancients had to understand mental illness."

"What do you mean?"

"Think about it. The scriptures never talk about 'depression' or 'anxiety' or people having 'obsessions.' Surely these things existed. How else could the ancients understand why a person with a healthy body was acting so strangely? Something bad, something evil, had gotten a hold of his spirit."

Jerome could see the point but was not convinced.

Father Mike went on. "Besides, the idea of an evil spirit also seemed to explain 'temptation'—why we *say* we know something is wrong but we do it anyway. Sometimes we say we can't help ourselves ... what, then, is pulling us? Today we explain things much more straightforwardly, pointing to things we experience all the time instead of an explanation based on something we never see. In the case of temptation, the two 'voices' have to do with the difference between what I want *RIGHT NOW* and what is good for me in the long run. Today we understand that even though a person says he *knows* something, he is never completely *sure*. The gap between thinking something ... hoping that it's true ... and being sure that it is going to bring you glory is the space in which sin takes place. Life is about growing in God's image and becoming more and more sure that you see what God sees.

"And one more thing," said Father Mike, "the idea of Satan in particular had the purpose of making evil personal. People are always more motivated to resist a bad person who is trying to hurt them rather than deal with 'imperfection' or 'the human struggle.' This is what people are doing when they see the devil in every detail, and say 'the devil uses good intentions,' and stuff like that. And we can see why! After all, 'I'm not going to let him get me' is much more motivating than thinking, 'Human nature is inherently imperfect,' or 'Doing great things is supposed to be difficult.'"

Jerome smiled.

"But," continued Father Mike, "this does not mean that there really is an evil being, an evil spiritual being roaming around the world trying to make life harder. Why, really, would God allow that?

"Why would He who loves us leave us at the mercy of such a creature?

"Why would any spiritual beings who saw God's face reject Him and become evil?

"Why, if He could share His life fully by creating spiritual beings directly, did He make *us*?"

"So," said Jerome, slightly changing the subject, "there are no angels either?"

"It's like with devils, Jerome. We are using a literary device in order to talk about something that's hard to talk about otherwise.

"In the case of angels, it has to do with needing to say that God communicated with people in detail, or did very specific things, without having to describe God and make Him too human.

"The word 'angel' means 'messenger,' and this was the idea.

"But, if God could share His life fully by creating spiritual beings directly, why did He make *us*?

"What happens to the deep and wonderful idea we now have about the purpose of our lives on earth?

"And there's an even deeper principle here," said Father Mike.

"Sometimes people think that you should give up on believing in something only if someone can 'prove' to you it *isn't* true.

"But that's not really being a mature thinker, Jerome. To be a mature thinker is to accept something only when there is sufficient reason to accept it.

"In the case of angels, which we *don't* need in order to make sense of faith, which are much more easily explained in terms of the way ancient people thought, isn't it better that we believe only what we have reason to believe, especially since reason has led us to an explanation of life, which is wonderful, and is even more scientific than science?!"

"So, we don't believe in the Bible anymore." Jerome's comment was really a question.

"We do believe, Jerome, that the Bible is the Word of God in a very special way.

"God inspired ... in other words, God's plan led to the writing of certain books and letters, and then it led to the Church's decision to accept these writings as holy and to assemble them into the collection we now call the Bible.

"These writings record for us the faith of the first Christians, and from their faith we can get to the information we need about the real life of Jesus, and his teachings, and his death, and his Resurrection.

"The Old Testament records the faith that Jesus started with.

"But God's plan used the humanity of these writers in order to translate His truth into terms their readers could understand. He did not 'possess' these writers. They were still people, and they had the job of becoming their own persons just like everyone else. And they and their readers were much simpler than most people today. Today, we have to remember that when we read what they wrote. This way we can interpret correctly God's message for *us*.

"You know, Jerome," continued Father Mike, "it was always necessary to interpret the Bible.

"People always saw that the Bible has lots of stories and lines that are not clear, or, if you take them literally, look wrong.

"I mean, is it right that to be a Christian you have to 'hate your mother and your father'?!

"You're not allowed to have two coats?!!

"Anybody not baptized is going to hell?!!!

"Besides, lines on a page can be read to say anything a person wants them to say. This certainly has happened over and over in Christian history.

"No, lines on a page do not interpret themselves. The scriptures have to be interpreted.

"This, by the way, is one of the reasons that God established a Church, and didn't just leave behind a book to guide us.

"The idea is this: by having official interpreters—who, as leaders of God's Church, are guided by His plan so that the Church will realize its destiny—we have an official interpretation that, at any given time, is the best the world can do *so far*.

"And by acknowledging the truth that exists in this interpretation, even if it is not the best explanation that might someday become official, all God's people can still embrace the same teachings. We can stay one.

"We can stay one, but we will continue to grow in our understanding of things, and our interpretations will get deeper. Growing, after all, is the reason we are here.

"And this is what we have been doing, for centuries.

"We have learned a lot, Jerome.

"We have learned that to explain their world and justify their rules, all ancient peoples told stories of fantastic things we never see happening today.

"We have learned that people love books, and they especially love holy books so they can hold the truth in their hands.

"Now, because we have grown, guided by Christianity for almost two thousand years, we have deeper ideas than the people of times past, including deeper ideas about God and His love, and the reason we are here, and why things happen.

"Now we understand that it is a mistake to presume to take ancient things literally!"

"So how do we know when we should and when we shouldn't?" asked Jerome.

"Well, there's a whole science about this, Jerome, but the short of it is: if our experience of God and our deepest, best ideas about life seem to be contradicted by something in the scriptures—and we are not just running away from a challenging truth!—we are probably right in NOT taking something literally but rather looking *within* the line or the story for something that *does* look true."

"What do you mean 'within'?"

"Stories and lines that are 'specific' contain several levels of truth that are more 'general.' Take, for example, the story of creation. You can take it as a story that tells what God did day by day for six days. Or you can take it as a story where the six days are not days but represent six longer periods of time ... and try to explain why the story says He created daylight and the next day He created the sun ... or you can take it as a story that was meant to say that God made everything. In the case of the story of creation, this is how far down we have to go until we find something we see as true." Father Mike paused. "But this is no problem."

"I think it *is* a problem," Jerome responded, "because now you are making the truth whatever you want."

"No, Jerome, not whatever we want. At every step of the way we have to show *why* we're saying what we're saying.

"For example, when we say that we can't take the story of creation literally, we can point to the overwhelming evidence that the world took a lot more than six days to go from nothing into being what it is today.

"It is true that when this first started to become obvious, people were upset. They thought, 'This means that what the Bible says isn't true.' But they kept thinking. They knew, for sure, that they still loved the faith they got from the Bible, especially the idea of God's love that they found in the story of Jesus. They knew that they needed the Bible to be the historical basis of what they believed about Jesus. And then they noticed that, for the sake of believing in the love of God, it doesn't really matter whether God created in six days, or sixty, or six billion years. What really matters ... what really matters to their faith ... is that God is ultimately the Creator of everything. And isn't this what the story tells, in a *storyteller's way*!? Wasn't this a good way to describe creation to people who were not scientific and didn't have the information we have today?!

"You see, Jerome," continued Father Mike, "by accepting the idea that God's truth was 'inside' the literal meaning of the words, the Church was able to affirm the truth that really matters to us without having to deny the facts of science and fall into that trap that we have always condemned—that we are believing what we want to believe!

"We ended up with a deeper idea of the Bible, and a better idea of creation, and grounds to keep insisting that reason is on our side. Just for listening to our faith—listening to what our faith tells us is really essential."

Jerome was listening. He was clearly conflicted.

Father Mike then added this: "But this way of looking at things ... it's not just for the story of creation. It's now the way we look at everything that was written a long time ago. People, a long time ago, had different—and we can say 'less sophisticated,' much more black and white—ideas than we do about many, many things. That's why if something to us today doesn't look right, we look inside it for a truth that does look right and strikes our faith as something that God wants us to see."

"Isn't that risky?" asked Jerome.

"I would say that it is necessary, Jerome. And I would say that we can trust our faith to guide us well. And then I would say that if the Church ultimately accepts what we come up with, we can be very confident that this is what God wants us to believe together."

"How can you be so sure what God wants you to believe?"

"Basically," Father Mike replied, "because I can show you. Did you come to both my talks?"

"Yes."

"Didn't you notice that at no time did I ever say that you have to believe this or that 'because it's in the Bible' or 'because the Church says so' or for any other reason that you could not check out for yourself?"

"I guess so."

"No, I never did. What I did do was try to explain things so that all of you could *see it for yourselves*. We started from the ground up—how we can experience God and how we know that this experience tells the truth. From there we went on to show how we know the truth of every other essential thing that we believe, from which come the core gifts of faith.

"Doing this is called 'apologetics,' from the Greek word for 'explanation.' This is the way we have to do it in the modern world. In the old days, there was one book and one voice of truth, and nobody else thought they knew anything. Now everybody feels free to have his or her own opinion, and many people talk to us about religion. They swear they know what they are talking about, and they seem sure, but they say different things, and many people are just plain confused. There is no way we will be able to get people to believe together, and to have a faith that will motivate them to do anything great, until we can explain things so that they can see it for themselves. I sure hope I am doing this for you!"

"Maybe. But it still seems a little dangerous. I mean when we had the Bible ... there it was."

"I guess, Jerome, it would be great if we didn't have to learn, didn't have to grow, didn't have to let things go. But this is just not the case. The faith of the ancients just won't work for us today. I do know that it is a little dangerous to feel free to speak differently about things we have always believed in a certain way. But we are talking about a specific beautiful idea of life, and super-clear reasons why we embrace it. And we don't ask anybody to see anything differently unless we can show them why."

"So did Jesus do any miracles?"

"One of the things about apologetics, Jerome, is that we don't say what we don't know."

"What do you mean?"

"Well," said Father Mike, "on one hand"—Father Mike held up his hand—"Jesus was *Jesus*, and we do have testimony that says he did some amazing things.

"On the other hand"—Father Mike held up his other hand—"we also know it was the ancients' way ... it is still the way for many people ... to prove things with miracle stories, mostly because they don't know how else to make a case.

"So, now that we have these two *hands*, we now have two ways to talk about these kind of stories. We have *tradition*"—Father Mike lifted higher his left hand—"and we have *doctrine*"—Father Mike lifted higher his right hand.

"Doctrine," explained Father Mike, "is what we know for sure.

"It's what we can verify in our experience, either directly, such as the idea that God made us for heaven, or because it is an implication of what we can verify directly, such as the Resurrection, which is an implication of the doctrine of the family that we can't do without."

Jerome was again conflicted. The argument sounded good—but he also felt that he was being asked to give up too much. He chose not to say this.

Father Mike continued. "Tradition, on the other hand, is tradition. It consists of stories that have been passed on, mostly from a long time ago.

"The idea that this or that actually happened, just as the story goes, is not essential to the truth of faith—the truth that gives the gifts of faith....

"Though there might some reason to believe a fantastic story—because almost everything has some historical basis—there is also good reason to question it. People believe in miracles much too easily. Pre-scientific people thought *everything* that they couldn't explain was a miracle. And today we realize that God's plan doesn't need miracles to accomplish God's purpose.

"And we shouldn't believe in anything without sufficient reason. That's what 'reason' is all about!"

Jerome was starting to look a little overwhelmed. But Father Mike had one more point to add: "Ideas from tradition aren't proofs because they don't prove. Too often they add, unnecessarily, to the things people think they are supposed to believe in."

"Is there going to be any kind of course so I can learn more about all this stuff," asked Jerome, "such as how to read the Bible and what is doctrine?"

"Well, Jerome, I have been invited to come back to your church for a course called 'Faith Takes You Seriously,' and I think I'm going to be able to do it. Listen for the announcement."

"I will. And I will come if you do it."

"Thank you," said Father Mike, and he gave Jerome this:

This is **My Bible Bookmark**.

I keep it in my Bible to remind myself of what the Bible is, and what it is not.

The Bible is a collection of books and letters that God inspired in order to provide His people with a basis for their faith.

The Bible is not a catechism, a religion textbook, or a handbook of truth that is meant to be read without prior knowledge or understanding.

The books and letters in the Bible were first intended to teach the truth to people of long, long ago. These people had much simpler ideas of almost everything we think about today.

This is the reason the Bible must always be interpreted from the point of view of what we know now. If we do not do this, many things will not make sense, and the Bible will seem to speak to us of a God so much less loving than we ourselves experience. ■

■

MARGARET
(WANTS TO KNOW
IF WE BELIEVE IN MARY)

Father Mike had not said anything to upset Margaret, who loves the Blessed Mother. He hadn't said anything at all about Mary, and this is what bothered her.

"How can we be Catholic if we don't believe in the Blessed Mother?" she wanted to know.

Father Mike replied, "Margaret, who said that we don't believe in the Blessed Mother?"

"You never mentioned her."

"That's true, Margaret, but I was talking about the most basic things. Our faith is big. And you can't talk about all the beautiful things it holds in a single speech."

"Isn't the Blessed Mother basic?"

"Actually, yes," said Father Mike, "but the reason we honor Mary is really *so* basic that it's not usually something we need to talk about."

"What do you mean?"

"The reason, Margaret, that Mary is so important in our faith is that Mary is the main example we have of someone who accepted the hard things the Father sent into her life. Even though she did not understand why, even though the trials did not seem fair, even though it was impossible to see what good could come from them, she accepted them, just because she trusted God. 'He knows better than I do.'"

Margaret nodded, tentatively.

"This is the story of Mary, who at the beginning of the Gospel is being asked to accept something that she could not have understood—but who still responded, 'Let it be done to me as you say.' Then, at the end of the Gospel ... certainly, Mary must have wondered, 'Why are these people torturing my son?'"

Margaret was still listening.

"No matter how we interpret the history behind all this, Margaret, tradition makes clear that Mary was remembered for her remarkable holiness, and her calm acceptance of hard things *even though she didn't understand them!*

"And we need Mary for this example," continued Father Mike, "because we don't get it from Jesus."

"What do you mean, that Jesus is not an example?!" Margaret had never heard anything like this. It almost seemed sinful to say it!

Father Mike moved quickly to explain. "Jesus, of course, is our *main* example of accepting hard things. He accepted the Cross, accepted death.

"But it is hard for us to imagine that Jesus didn't know why this was happening. Jesus understood. He understood envy. He understood the need to back up your words with actions. In a sense he *wanted* to give his life for his mission.

"Mary wasn't thinking of any of these things. Mary was a simple, loving mother. She loved her son and did not understand why other people hated him. To lose him seemed like the worst thing that could possibly happen. But if God wanted her to bear it, she would bear it. This is the example of Mary, the reason that Mary is so important to the Church.

"And if you think of it, Margaret, you might notice that Mary's example is, in a way, even more important than the example of Jesus. It is for me. In my life, very few times have I had to accept something hard because I was doing good. Usually, when I do good—or, at least, try to—people thank me. For me, so often when I have to accept something hard, the thing *is* hard because it makes no sense. *I have so much to offer; why are they not listening? Everyone is waiting; why is there traffic?* For me, most of the time I have to accept things after the example of Mary."

"Is that all we believe about Mary?" asked Margaret.

"I think it's a lot, Margaret. And I have to tell you, far too often, what I see is that people get devotion to Mary backward."

"What do you mean?"

"I mean that rather than follow Mary's example and accept hard things—or at least accept that we need to deal with hard things—Mary is the main person we pray to when we want *to get out of hard things!*"

This stung Margaret just a bit. She did not show it.

Father Mike went on. "If you came to my first talk, Margaret, you may remember that I said that when it comes to faith, most people get it backward. They think that faith means that if you 'really believe' that God will do what you ask, then He will. When people say that they 'believe in' someone or something, spiritually speaking, it means that this is the person they call ... this is the thing they do ... in order to ask God for what they want. But that is not faith, faith in God, faith that God is God and He knows what He's doing, and faith that He's always doing what's best for us forever. And as we also said, when we have real faith, we get real peace. This is what we are supposed to get for following the example of Mary."

Now Margaret spoke up. "But Mary was special. Mary conceived without sin. Or don't we believe that anymore, either?"

"We believe, Margaret—and it is obvious that we are right—that from the moment of her conception, God's plan was preparing Mary perfectly to be the mother that Jesus needed.

"We know that Mary's holiness was the main human influence on the man who Jesus grew up to be.

"But Mary was born a baby; she undoubtedly cried for her milk, acted a little silly sometimes, and struggled with all sorts of human temptations.

"Nonetheless, from the moment of her conception, God's plan was preparing Mary perfectly to be mother that Jesus needed, a person of extraordinary holiness."

"So did Mary have other children?" asked Margaret. "Some people say she did."

"*Some people* should not declare that they know," replied Father Mike.

"The historical evidence is not clear.

"But I can tell you this: Mary was a heroically holy young woman and committed no sexual or other sin in her life.

"The conception of Jesus was special, planned by God to make Jesus the most special person who ever lived.

"No other children who maybe lived in that house in Nazareth were other Sons or Daughters of God with a big S or a big D.

"And if there were other kids in the house, it doesn't change a thing ... it doesn't change our essential faith in Jesus or Mary."

"And the Assumption?" asked Margaret.

"If you are asking, Margaret, is Mary in heaven body and soul, the answer is yes, absolutely.

"But then I might ask you, what does it mean that Mary has a body in heaven?"

Margaret wanted to say, "I thought you were the one who was supposed to tell me," but she did not.

Father Mike did not leave the question hanging for long. "Certainly we realize that, in heaven, we will have no use for a body like we have here—made of cells, walking on two feet held to the ground by gravity. Will we walk on the 'ground' of heaven?"

Margaret had never thought about this before, but still she knew that the answer was no.

Father Mike continued. "No, when we say that Mary has a body in heaven, and that we will, too, what we mean is that she and we will keep our individual identities. We will be transformed and exist in a form far greater than we had here, but I will still be me and you will still be you. Who we will be will be built on our memories.

"You might have heard life after death described like a drop in the bucket. In other words, if you drop a drop of water into a bucket of water, it does not retain its individual identity.

"We say this is impossible because, if this were the way things went, we would have no reason to strive for our eternal future, and creation itself would not work!"

"I guess not," said Margaret.

"Besides this," continued Father Mike, "the idea that we will each have a body in heaven helps us to understand that we will recognize one another in heaven—and much more than that. I do hope you understand that our whole idea of 'salvation' is based on the idea that we will be together and love each other much more intimately than we ever could here."

"I think I got that," said Margaret. But she knew she had a lot to think about. Finally she asked, "Is it wrong to say the Rosary?"

"Of course not," replied Father Mike immediately. "The Rosary has been a treasure in the Church for centuries *for a reason*. It is a simple, concrete way to pray. Its repetition helps us focus on God, and then to relax a little and to meditate—whether or not you do Rosary meditations with the decades. And repeating the Hail Mary, fifty-three times! This is a wonderful thing to do as long as we are clear about why we are doing it.

"If we are just asking and asking and asking, because the more we ask, the better chance that we will get what we are begging for—not so helpful.

"But if we are honoring Mary over and over again for her example of acceptance, we will teach ourselves to try to do the same. We will teach ourselves to see things as God does. And we will feel peace."

Father Mike decided to risk this: "You know, Margaret, I use a Hail Mary that is a little different, one that is designed to make devotion to Mary clearer and more effective. I say this:

> Blessed are you, Mary, because you accepted
> what you did not understand, solely because
> the Father sent it. May I, too, like you, trust
> Him.

"Can I get a copy of that?" asked Margaret.

"Of course," said Father Mike, "I have one right here." ∎

■

NICK
(WANTS TO KNOW
IF JESUS WAS GOD)

Nick was like Margaret. He came to Father Mike because of what he had *not* heard. Like Jerome, he was not angry but edgy.

"Father," he said, "I heard you talk about the Cross but I didn't hear you say anything about how Jesus died to save us from our sins."

"True, Nick," replied Father Mike, "but that was because I was trying to keep things simple—and the idea that Jesus died to save us from our sins takes a good bit of explaining if it is to make sense to us *today*."

"What do you mean?"

"Well, Nick, this idea was *always* a difficult thing to understand. I mean, it is easy to get the idea of ransom, and somebody giving up his life to save someone else. But normally we are paying this ransom to somebody bad! So why, then, would the Father want such a thing; and why would He want it from the pain of His Son?"

"Okay, why?" asked Nick.

"Tradition said that it was a demand of justice, that somebody had to make up for the sin of Adam, which corrupted human nature and led to the sins of all his descendants.

"And since his descendants—we—were stuck in sin and unworthy to make up for anything, the Father had to send His Son."

Nick nodded at this familiar formulation.

Father Mike went on. "But there were still problems. After all, God is the author of justice; He is not bound by it."

"What does that mean?"

"It means, Nick, that there is no power greater than God that makes Him carry out what, *to us*, are the demands of justice.

Besides," added Father Mike, "we now know that justice is not some system of rules that have to be followed whether I love you or not. Justice, in fact, is an inferior form of love."

"Could you explain that?"

"Sure," replied Father Mike. "Our sense of justice is something that emerges in us as we grow up. We grow into recognizing that other people *are* people just like us, and they have 'rights' to their stuff, and if they do something for us, we 'owe' them.

"And if we violate people's rights, or don't give them what we owe them, then we should be punished.

"Of course, if we do good for them, we should be rewarded.

"This is justice.

"But if we keep growing, and we come to see the depth and beauty in other people, in their spirits, in their souls ... then we start to care about them, not because we owe them but because they are who they are.

"This is the beginning of love.

"And love also involves forgiveness, because if you see the beauty in people's souls, you see goodness even if they've done bad things.

"You sometimes see that they have learned from sins—selfish things they've done.

"Because you know their souls were made of goodness, you always see that they have done the best they could with what they were given.

"That's love."

"So it's wrong to punish people?" asked Nick.

"Not if we are talking about raising children or managing society ... then we need punishments ... so kids will learn ... to protect people from criminals.

"But God ... *loves*. And if He wanted to forgive Adam and fix creation, He could have just done it.

"Am I being clear?"

"Clear, I guess so," said Nick, "but all that does is create more questions."

"Well," said Father Mike, "let me make things worse—and then we can make them better."

Nick did not know what to make of that.

Father Mike continued. "The whole idea, Nick, that the world is messed up and everyone is sinful because of Adam, the first man ... based on what you know about history, do you really see this happening?

"The idea that one man's mistake ruined creation—does this sound like a good way to make the universe?

"Was it fair—was it 'just'—to everybody who came after?

"By the way, did anybody ask to be born, and risk not doing what God wants and then what?"

"So are you saying that everything we believe is wrong?" asked Nick.

"Not at all," replied Father Mike. "To be truthful, I want to say that what we believe is right.

"The whole network of ideas that tradition passed to us—Adam's 'original' sin that corrupted the universe, the need for the Son of God to die for us, and all the rest of these traditional doctrines— were the very best God's people could do in order to understand why the world made by a good God was filled with evil, and why Jesus, who was so good, had to die in such a terrible way—and so on."

Nick was listening carefully.

Father Mike continued. "For us—now, not only is it hard for us to imagine a garden of paradise, not only do we not see any sign of such a thing and instead see all kinds of signs that primitive people were, well, *primitive*, and hardly capable of making any creation-shattering decisions, besides all this, our imagination now informs us that what we want from life with God is much more than we could ever have had in a garden of paradise."

"What do you mean?"

"We want to *see God*, Nick," answered Father Mike. "This eye will never do it." Father Mike pointed to his own. "We want to live forever. It is the nature of this body"—Father Mike grabbed his own arm—"not to. We expect the intimate union of all God's people. This could never happen here.

"Besides," Father Mike added. "If Adam hadn't sinned and no one had ever died, wouldn't the world have filled up a long time ago?"

"Wow," thought Nick. And then he asked, "So, why are we here?"

"So God could give us more than He could give us just creating us in heaven. We've talked about it a couple of times, lately, at your church.

"We are here, before heaven, so we can be involved in our creation ... to become people that *we* made *us* to be, because it is better for us if we are.

"People of the past did not think of this because their imaginations were smaller. They thought God's 'kingdom' was like a kingdom here, only nicer, 'cause God was king.

"Only lately have we come to understand that what we want—what God made us to want—is not possible here. And that's when we had to figure out what we are doing here."

"So why is there evil?" asked Nick.

"Because of why we are here. We are here to participate in our creation. But for this to happen, God had to make us and the world imperfect. If He had made us and the world perfect ... what does 'perfect' mean? Perfect means that something is all that it can be. If God had made us perfect, we would already be all that we could be and then we could not grow; we could not participate in our own creation.

"And 'imperfect' means *imperfect*—stuff we really *don't* want.

"This is the reason that we are born unformed, and ignorant, and utterly selfish. This is the reason we can make mistakes and become misguided. This is the reason we can be hurt. And when we *are* hurt, we suffer."

"*Why* do we have to suffer?" Nick needed to know more.

"Basically," said Father Mike, "suffering makes us real."

"What do you mean?"

"If nothing hurt, or dealt us something we *really* didn't want, we would have no reason to strive for something better. If things weren't sometimes *really* hard, we would have no reason to dig down deep and find out what we *really* believe, and make ourselves somebody that *we* made.

"And that, again, is the purpose of life."

"So how did Jesus save us from our sins?"

"Listen," said Father Mike, "why are we here ... to become somebody that *we* made. And how do we do that ... by growing in love. And growing *in* love is growing *out* of what ... selfishness; and selfishness is sin.

"And what inspires people to grow out of selfishness?" With this one, Father Mike paused. Then he said, "What pulls people out of selfishness is receiving love, and seeing good example. That's a big part of what Jesus did by dying on the Cross.

"Showing us that we are loved, and showing us that love means sacrifice ... by doing this, Jesus pulled us out of selfishness. In this sense, he saved us from our sins.

"So," said Father Mike, "to answer your question, 'How did Jesus save us from our sins?' He did what he had to do to create for us a path to a richer life with God forever.

"And traditional doctrines explained this in the only way that people of times past could understand it."

Father Mike went on. "But in our times, people can understand things better. They *need* to understand things better. Many ancient ideas no longer make sense to us. We want deeper ideas. And God has guided the Church to provide them, and, truthfully, our new ideas glorify God even more than our old ideas ever could!"

Nick needed a couple of seconds to process all this. Then he asked, "So was Jesus God?"

"Wow," said Father Mike. "There's a big question. Let me see if I can give you a good answer."

Almost simultaneously, each of them took a deep breath. Father Mike began, "It was a problem from the beginning.

"Believers have always felt that when they are looking at Jesus they are looking at God.

"But Jesus himself talked about God, God the Father. He prayed to the Father. He accepted the Father's will.

"He spoke of his *Father*, making himself God's *Son*.

"So, somehow, Jesus is *divine*, from God's own 'flesh,' from God's own *being*.

"But it was also people's experience that Jesus was human, not some sort of super-being faking humanity the way an alien in a movie can fake being human. This has always been important to Christians—that Jesus is one of us for real, God's Son but our brother. This is what makes everything Jesus went through so important, so inspirational.

"So the Church tried to put together the very different things that we knew about Jesus: Jesus is divine, but He is not the Father; and Jesus is also human.

"What the Church decided was this: before time, God the Father 'extended' Himself.

"What this means is that the Father gave over, or 'diverted,' or 'dedicated,' some of His infinite self and willed that there be another person.

"Crudely you might picture this in terms of a bunch of clay—the clay is the divine 'stuff'—and God gave over a big piece of it so that something else could exist. Actually," qualified Father Mike quickly, "this example is not excellent because there really is no divine 'stuff' that God is made of. If there were some stuff that God is made of, you could ask the question, 'Who made that?!' No, the divine 'stuff' is God Himself—there is no difference between who God is and what He is made of. In giving existence to 'something else,' God really is giving of Himself.

"And you might notice, Nick," added Father Mike, "that this makes God's parenthood much more giving than anything we can do. We give some of the stuff in our bodies and this grows into someone else. We do not give our 'selves.' God did.

"Are you still with me?"

"Keep going," said Nick.

Father Mike kept going. "So the basic idea is that Jesus is God *but not all of Him.*"

"I guess I can see that," said Nick.

"Do you also see that everything I just described looks a lot like what we said when we talked about the Cross—when I tried to explain that one of the meanings of the Cross is that we are made of God's love—that each of us is made of God but not all of Him?!"

"So we are sons of God, too?" asked Nick.

"We *are* sons and daughters of God, Nick. We are made in His image, resembling Him in a holistic way."

But before Nick could ask, Father Mike answered.

"When I say that we resemble God in a 'holistic' way, I mean that *not* like a rock or a tree; we resemble the aspect of God that *does* things, makes decisions, loves, etc., the greatest things about God that we know of.

"And we, too, are the products of God love, conceived by Him from all eternity."

Now Nick asked, "So there is no difference between Jesus and us?"

"There is a big difference," replied Father Mike. "Jesus was *the* Son, the only One, sent to teach the rest of us who we are. He was *the* Son who would speak for the Father and call us to be His family. He was *the* Son whose life was planned to speak for God as nothing else does, and in whose face we could see the face of the Father as nowhere else."

"So where does the Holy Spirit come in?" asked Nick.

Father Mike answered right away. "Just as the Son is God as He is present in Jesus, the Holy Spirit is God as He is present in the rest of creation, sustaining it, and guiding it, and in the design of our human nature, so that we can experience the Father when we think and when we pray.

"But," interjected Father Mike, "this experience, that God is in me but this presence is not the person of the Father or the person of the Son ... this experience led the Church to put into words the doctrine of the Trinity, the idea that in God there are three Persons.

"Basically," said Father Mike, "this is how it happened: The Church knows that God is our Father. That's Person Number One. The Church sees God when she looks at Jesus—but Jesus is always talking about the Father. This makes Jesus Person Number Two. And the Church feels God inside the faithful— but this presence is pointing people toward Jesus and the Father. This Holy Spirit, the same Holy Spirit that all of us share, is Person Number Three.

"But," continued Father Mike, "the Church was still sure that God is One, in other words, there is only one God, and in an absolutely undividable way, He is One unified being.

"Trying to put all this together became the doctrine of the Trinity.

"And now we know that the Church was able to come up with the doctrine of the Trinity because it already, if vaguely, possessed the deepest idea of God that anyone ever had—the idea that God is more than one person as you or I are each only one person.

"If you came to my talks, Nick, I hope you saw how we showed that God *is* more than one person as you or I are one person—because He made so many things, such as romance, that require the participation of more than one person—and how super useful is this idea in explaining why He made a family with whom to share His life, and that we are going to share God's life *as* a family, etc."

"I did get that," said Nick.

There was a slight lull.

"I'm going to need some time to think about all this," said Nick. "But I do have one more question, for now."

"Please," said Father Mike.

"I heard what you said about how Communion is the Body of Christ."

"Okay."

"But I remember being taught that Communion really is Jesus. Do we still believe that?"

Father Mike again smiled. "You do like big questions."

This time Nick smiled, too.

"Okay," said Father Mike, sort of revving up. "Let's start with this. Jesus, the person; where is he now?"

"Heaven." Nick seemed unsure if he were answering or asking.

"Good," said Father Mike, "but you also know that a person 'in heaven' is really 'with God' and God is everywhere."

"That makes sense."

"This means that Jesus is everywhere."

"Sure."

"But we cannot focus on 'everywhere.' We cannot pay attention to God's presence if we are asked to do so in everything, in every direction, and in the air around things, and in our eyes, all the time!

"For this reason God ordained a place where He wants us to see and touch Him.

"In this special way, He stands behind this place. He is uniquely present there for just this reason.

"Does this make sense?"

"Not sure," said Nick.

"Take your time and think about things," suggested Father Mike. "If you have more questions, or if something just doesn't make sense, write it down! Come back. We can talk some more."

"I can do that," replied Nick.

"And one more thing, Nick. You have great questions; and I am sure that you will understand our faith better for every second you put into it. I really suggest reading." And with that Father Mike gave Nick his guide to theological reading. ■

◧

AL
(WANTS TO KNOW
IF WHAT HE'D BEEN TAUGHT
WAS WRONG IS NOW ALL RIGHT)

Al was afraid that he was going to look stupid. He wanted to talk to Father Mike, but not about anything Father Mike had dealt with in the talks he had attended. He wanted to talk about his divorce.

"I just don't know what to think," he said.

"Explain to me the problem," said Father Mike, "and let's see what we can do."

"Okay," said Al. "I was married at twenty-two. It was okay for a while, but soon enough we noticed that we really didn't agree about anything. We had a couple of kids.

"I've tried to be a good father to them, even from a distance.

"We hung in for the kids. It was really over after about six years. We finally separated and divorced after nine.

"I was fine being alone for a while. I never felt desperate to find somebody else. I didn't think I ever would.

"My wife, my wife *now* ... we started out as friends. It's funny, but the main thing we had in common was faith. We were both raised Catholic and liked church. She was never married. We got married civilly—and, of course, we stopped going to Communion. But we never stopped going to church. And, of course, we felt bad, we *feel* bad, when it's time for Communion and we just sit there. It's not that we think people are looking—but they probably are—but you know, in our church the priest is always talking about Communion.

"He has this really good example. He says that a piece of paper is just a piece of paper; but if you write 'I love you' on it, now it's so much more. He says that that's what the blessing does for the bread.

"And we just sit there and don't receive it."

Father Mike just nodded.

"So here comes my brother," continued Al. "He moved away a long time ago. But almost the exact same thing happens to him—he gets divorced, then remarries—and he goes to his church, meets with the priest in his parish a few times, and they tell him it's okay if he goes to Communion.

"I just don't know what to think."

"I can see why, Al," said Father Mike. "Did you go to your pastor to talk about this?"

"I did go, and the priest talked to me about an annulment, but that didn't seem right."

"Why not?"

"Because the idea of it—that you should swear that you didn't really know what you were doing when you got married, that you didn't really know what a commitment was really all about, that somebody had some kind of psychological 'block' about being in a commitment, that kind of stuff ... it just wasn't honest. I mean we were immature and all that—but who isn't? We knew what a commitment was, and we wanted to make it. It just didn't work out."

"Did anyone ever talk to you about an 'internal forum' solution to your problem?"

"Internal what?

"Internal forum. It means 'private.' It really has to do with the sacrament of Confession."

"I never heard of it."

"The idea is actually pretty simple. You know that you could kill somebody tomorrow, go to Confession, and go to Communion the next day."

"I guess so."

"So why can't we also forgive a failed marriage?"

"Why?"

"Traditionally, the idea was that if you kill someone, this person is dead. There's no way to fix it. But if you divorce someone, there is always the possibility that you can be reconciled. If we forgive your divorce, we are telling you that you don't have to try anymore to keep the promise you made. If we say it's okay to marry someone else we, the Church, are killing the commitment you once made before God."

"I can see that."

"Yes, but in today's world, we are capable of observing that even though two people are still alive, their marriage can be dead."

Al was listening intently. Father Mike went on. "In times past, it was not so easy to see this. After all, what was marriage? Marriage was an agreement to live together for better or worse—but it was mostly worse. Most people's lives were a drudgery, and there wasn't much to be gained leaving one bum to live with another."

Al smiled. Father Mike went on. "Only lately have things changed. Only lately are many people capable of sharing an intimacy and a rich life together that in earlier times was rare for married couples. But this also means that there is more that can go wrong.

"Not only is there more that can go wrong, but we are living in the first generation in the history of the world where temptations come at you from everywhere, and people feel freer than ever to go their own ways.

"Obviously marriage was going to suffer—and it has.

"But the Church understands this. And the Church is now able to distinguish between a situation where a person *refuses* to keep his or her promise, and a situation where he or she *cannot* keep the promise."

There was a pause. Father Mike went on. "Suppose I tell you ... I swear to you,' after our meeting I am going to take you out for a hamburger.' And then our meeting ends, and we go outside, and my car doesn't start. I'm not going to take you for a hamburger, but this does not mean I broke my promise. It's not that I don't want to, it's that I can't. This is the real situation of many broken marriages.

"Marriage takes two. The human heart is fragile. Sometimes things happen and a marriage dies. And we can be morally certain that it is not coming back. I see this all the time."

"You're seeing it now," said Al.

Father Mike continued. "But I also see that when people have been through something difficult, they learn. They learn about life; they learn about love; they grow. And this hardly makes them *less* in need of companionship.

"They fall in love again—or, in most cases, for the first time for real. Of course they are sincere about a commitment. Of course they want God's blessing ... but what do they do?"

Al knew this was not a question for him, at least not yet.

Father Mike continued. "They come to the Church. They get help to examine their hearts and their intentions. And if they can in conscience present their new marriage to God as something they are committed to keep holy, they can receive forgiveness for what came before.

"The Church does not allow a second 'public' wedding, which would certainly confuse the idea that when a couple makes a promise to God, it is meant to last for life; but in human situations, when forgiveness is right, forgiveness is given, and people are invited back to Communion, and they can look at their marriage as God really sees it. Am I being clear?"

"Wow," said Al. "But I have to ask you."

"Please," said Father Mike.

"Isn't all this just diluting the rules, God's rules?"

"It would be, Al, if we were saying yes to you even though we knew we were hurting the institution of marriage and planting the seeds of many other people's suffering.

"But this is not at all the case.

"Forgiveness in private for you is simply commonsense compassion.

"It does not mean that we have changed our ideals, and what we are working for all the time.

"But with regard to marriage, you don't get marriages to last by making more rules; you get marriages to last by inspiring people to love.

"We're still working on that—and we're NOT contradicting the cause by being compassionate to you."

"So we *bend* the rules?" asked Al.

"It's not about bending rules, Al," said Father Mike. "It's about rethinking the idea of rules and what they're for."

Father Mike took a breath. Al thought he saw a speech coming.

"Let's start at the beginning," began Father Mike, "with the purpose of life. If you came to my talks, you know that the purpose of life is to prepare to share God's life, and that we do this by growing in love as best we can and helping others to do the same.

"This is the one absolute rule that we have, Al, the one rule we always follow in every situation. It's our answer to the question, what is love? What is going to advance the cause of love in the world?

"No other rule is absolute because no other rule— no other single sentence—can adequately account for every possible situation.

"Every other rule does the best it can to tell us what we should normally do, or normally strive for, to advance the cause of love.

"But real life creates exceptions.

"There are times when to insist on what we normally do, to insist on the ideal, will hurt people—and do nothing good for the world.

"When we suspect this, we ask ourselves, what is the goal of the rule?

"Will this exception ... this kind of exception, defeat this goal? If we create a precedent for this kind of exception, in the long run, will the world suffer?

"Or is the precedent safe because special cases are clearly special and do not involve people selfishly declaring themselves free from a rule they would want others to follow?

"Is the precedent safe because of how we administer it, not celebrating what should not be celebrated but simply showing compassion for something that is not intrinsically harmful or selfish, and may instead be love?"

"How?" Al had a sense of what this might mean, and he wanted to hear it.

Father Mike went on. "In other words, Al, does forgiveness for your first, failed marriage hurt the institution of marriage in the eyes of people who will one day marry? Or is welcoming you and your wife back to Communion helping you to keep alive the real love you are trying to live faithfully?"

"But what about what Jesus said about divorce—and if you get a divorce and marry somebody else you are committing adultery?" Al was expressing his every doubt!

"Well," said Father Mike, "don't we have a quote from the same Jesus saying that if you look twice at a woman who is not your wife you are committing adultery?"

"I guess."

"And do you really think that God wants us to see this as the same thing as sleeping with someone who is not your wife?"

"I guess not."

"See, Al," said Father Mike, "what Jesus is doing in the Gospel is what we often do when we are exhorting people to holiness—we use words in a black-and-white way. It's the same thing that Jesus was doing when we read that to be his disciple we have to hate our mothers and our fathers and not have two coats!

"Here are the bottom lines: God does want marriage to be for life. He does not want anyone to feel free, for a selfish reason, to write his wife a 'divorce letter' and go out and look for someone new.

"God wants us to give our all to make our marriage work—and for each of us to 'do all that I can do, and not to quit because I decide that he or she is not trying as hard as I am.'

"But the whole teaching of Jesus, which is all about compassion and not being bound by all kinds of absolute rules, should make clear to us that God understands our failures, forgives us, and does not want us to be punished for the rest of our lives—especially when there is nothing to be gained by it!"

"I have one more question."

"Please."

"Was I a fool to obey the law and stay away from Communion all these years?"

"Absolutely not, Al. Every single Sunday, when you obeyed what you were taught, you made a sacrifice that was an act of faith. Every single time this made you—and Mrs. Al—grow in holiness. Come back to see me again, and bring her."

"I will." ■

■

DONNA
(CANNOT AFFORD
TO HAVE ANY MORE CHILDREN)

Donna told Father Mike that she had enjoyed his first two talks; she'd never known that faith was so simple—but deep, and beautiful—and that it offered so much. But for these same reasons, faith had never been so challenging. This meant that she was now bothered by a decision she had hardly thought twice about when she'd first made it. She asked Father Mike to talk with her.

"We already had two children," she said. "And I was already thirty, and for every reason in the book, we were happy with our family and we really didn't think we could handle any more. We didn't want to," Donna admitted.

"So I went on the Pill. I heard that the Church was against it," said Donna, "but I didn't know anybody else who had a problem with it. And I couldn't see what the problem was. So I really didn't think twice about it.

"Now I am coming to church more. I like what I'm hearing, and so I am thinking, 'If you're right about what I like, then ...'"

"Wow," said Father Mike, "that is really honest of you. And I am really happy we can talk about this."

He now asked Donna a question: "When you decided to have your first child," he asked, "what were you hoping for?"

"Wow," said Donna, "I didn't expect to be asked that." It took a moment but then Donna said, "Well, I guess it just seemed like the right thing to do."

"Why?"

Another unexpected question. It took another moment, but then Donna said, "I guess we thought it would be beautiful. You have a baby who needs you. You watch her grow; you help her grow; she gets to have some of the good things we had."

"Church jargon says, 'You give life as life was given to you,'" said Father Mike. "Does that sound right?"

"Very."

"Church jargon also says, 'The life you give gets to live forever; what could be better than that?' How does that sound?"

"Even better."

"Okay, Donna. Did you think it was going to be easy, being a mom?"

"Oh no. I have an older sister. She'd already had three kids."

"So you knew that it was going to be a big sacrifice?"

"Well, maybe not as big as it was!"

"But then you decided to do it again."

"Well, yes. We were hoping for a boy, and we didn't think it would be good for our daughter to be an only child."

"That's the reason?"

"Oh no. We knew that when he was born we would love him—and we did. And we do!"

"Not a surprise," said Father Mike. "I am asking you these questions, Donna, because I need us to be clear about the right reason to have *any* children. How could we talk sensibly about the decision not to have any *more* children until we were clear about that?"

"That makes sense."

"And I wanted to be sure the right reason to have children makes sense, because it's the right reason that makes all the sacrifices acceptable, and the risks you accept when you have kids, and the fact that once you have given them all you can, they leave you!"

This brought a wry smile to Donna's lips.

Father Mike continued. "This is the main thing the Church teaches," he said, "that people who love each other, and who are committed to love each other all their lives, have an opportunity to do just about the most divine thing we can imagine: to give life as life was given to them, life that gets to live with God forever. And as we always add, 'What could be better than that?'

"Now," continued Father Mike, "in the old days ... if it's so good to do this, you do it! You have as many kids as you possibly can.

"And that wasn't just a theory. People had practical reasons, too, to have as many kids as they could. Kids were a poor person's riches. They were workers for the farm. 'Somebody to take care of me *when* I get old.' And let's not forget, in times past, many children died. Parents needed as many as they could get.

"But things have changed. Today most people don't have farms—and having kids is very expensive. Also, people have other ways to manage when they get old. And now, at least here, most kids live to be adults.

"The human spirit has changed, too." Father Mike had clicked into a speech he had given many times before. "As the human family has accomplished more, people expect more from life. They want more from life, many things that the people of times past couldn't even have imagined. And raising babies is only one of the good things that people can do to make the world a richer place.

"That's why many people started to want to plan their families—and who else should plan for them?! Like nothing else, having kids is a lifelong sacrifice. You're not going to do it well unless you choose it, unless you choose it freely—and joyfully. And who else knows the factors you are weighing when it's time to make your decisions?

"Bottom line: it's your choice.

"The question is, *how* do we plan our families?"

Donna had not noticed that it had taken a while to get to her question.

"I think, Donna," said Father Mike, "that here the Church has done a pretty poor job of making itself clear. The Church is in the business of offering teachings to help people manage major life issues. This, of course, is right. Faith is our explanation of life. How could our explanation of life not have something to do with the issue of transmitting life?

"Now, when it comes to the means of family planning—a major life issue, for sure—the Church wants to point out to people that there is a natural way to do it. There is a natural way to it that involves no expenses, no operations, no playing with the chemistry of a woman's body, no artificial anything getting in between the two people—and this is a way that does not require people to do something less than the act of love for all it can be.

"And thanks to modern science, the same science that brought us the Pill, when a woman knows how to read the signs in her body ... the signs that indicate that she can conceive, she might discover that her fertile period is as little as a few days a month.

"And, by the way," said Father Mike smiling, trying not to embarrass Donna, "even during that day, or during that week, there are other ways that couples can please each other that sometimes are more special because they allow one person to pay more attention to the other person, and vice versa."

Father Mike continued. "The Church points out that not only are artificial methods artificial but they are hardly foolproof, and they fool people into taking 'chances' that they do not know they are taking. What is worse, they sometimes give people the idea that they have some kind of guarantee that they will not get pregnant, and this is not good when the time comes to accept a child that *is* coming, planned or not.

"But here's the big problem with artificial methods. Some work by sometimes inducing an abortion."

This statement gave Donna a start.

"IUDs sometimes do this," said Father Mike, "and so does the Pill."

Father Mike could see that Donna was getting upset. "Please understand, Donna, I'm not saying— science doesn't say—that IUDs and the Pill *always* work this way. Most times they don't—by far. But think of it this way, would you allow a child to play with a bomb that *probably* wouldn't go off—only one chance in a hundred?

"The way I like to explain it is like this. Some artificial methods are always wrong because they sometimes work by inducing an abortion. Some methods don't involve this possibility—barrier methods, for example, and some creams. But these still have their downside. On the other hand, humanly speaking, some people may need time to get comfortable with reading bodily signs. Also, for some women, their time of true desire is always too close to their fertile period, or their fertile period is much longer than most. And this is information nobody else has, and nobody needs to judge for them.

"So what am I saying? I like to say that the methods of family planning form a 'continuum' that goes from things that are always right to things that are always wrong, and there are a number of things in the middle. That's where it's up to you. What do you think?"

"I think my husband is in for a surprise." ■

◘

MATT
(HAS A DIFFICULT
DECISION TO MAKE)

Matt had not come to Father Mike's first talk. But he'd heard enough about it to think, "Maybe this guy can help me figure things out." So he went to that second talk and thought that this *was* a guy who could help him figure things out. He made an appointment, and here he was.

"How can I help?" asked Father Mike.

"I have a situation," replied Matt. He was prepared and so went right into his story. "I've been working for these people for years," he said, "and I'm not going to say who they are," he continued, "because I want to keep you out of it.

"It took a while," Matt went on, "before I figured out what was going on. Basically, they're stealing. They're ripping off at least a dozen of their clients.

"They're selling defective materials ... eventually somebody is gonna get hurt, bad.

117

"But these guys don't care; and they're gonna keep stealing.

"I tell myself, 'Their clients are probably rich, and maybe nobody will get hurt.' But I know this is not my call; and I know what they're doing is not right."

"What are your options, Matt?"

"This is the problem. If I say anything to them— then they're gonna know I know. They're not gonna do anything about it—they're just gonna fire me. And then if I report them ... you gotta know these people ... they're dangerous."

"No chance to do something anonymously?" asked Father Mike.

"It won't work," said Matt. "First of all, they're *gonna* know who called. And no investigation is getting anywhere unless I tell them what I saw.

"I thought about just leaving," continued Matt, "but nobody is hiring right now—not for what I do— and they're not gonna be hiring for who knows how long, the way things are. And I'm up to my neck. I have a mortgage. I have a family. I can miss a paycheck, maybe a month, but after that we're not eating.

"And not just me. A lot of innocent people are gonna get hurt if these people go down—and some of them are in worse shape than I am.

"And even if I just left, and took any other kind of job, and took a chance I wouldn't be able to support my family, I would still know those people were ripping off their clients ... and somebody is probably gonna get hurt. I just don't know what to do," Matt said.

Father Mike asked a few more questions. He was hoping that there was some way out that maybe Matt hadn't thought of. Unfortunately, there didn't appear to be. Finally, Father Mike took a deep breath and said, "Wow. This is a tough one. Let me try to lay it out the way I believe God sees it.

"First of all," said Father Mike, "I thank you for coming. You didn't say it, but you could have chosen to do nothing and not even considered this mess a moral matter. This is a great statement about your faith and your love for people you don't even know.

"But," continued Father Mike, "what do we do? What do *I* do if I am going to tell you the truth about how I believe God sees this?

"The first thing I need to say is that you didn't make it easy!

"Sometimes when people come to speak about a moral decision, I get an easy way out.

"Sometimes I get to give the other person an easy way out because, really and truly, the problem is not their problem.

"Sometimes it's really not their business to get involved in somebody else's business. It's not their responsibility, and they would be doing more harm than good if they try to *make it* their responsibility.

"Sometimes they've already done their duty. They've said what they needed to say, offered what they needed to offer, or already tried their realistic best, and it didn't work ... and now they have to allow other people to make their choices and deal with what they chose.

"Sometimes there is a 'compromise' solution—a way to make things right without getting 'caught.'"

"I wish," interjected Matt.

"Me too," said Father Mike. "But I can see that there isn't. So this is what I have to say ... this is what I *have to* say, Matt; this is what I feel obligated to say:

"Faith's way is always to do the right thing, no matter what. Faith says that this is always worth it, whatever it costs.

"Faith says that we are here to get ready to be who we are going to be *forever*. Faith says that the more we grow in faith and love, the more like God we become, the greater will be our lives with God when finally we get to see Him.

"Faith says that we are in this together and if I help others do better ... not get ripped off, etc. ... the greater will be the life that all of us will share.

"Faith says that the greater the challenge, the greater the opportunity to do more with this one life that we were given.

"And faith says that the way to glory is to follow Jesus even if it means ... *especially* if it means that we have to, in any sense, give up our lives.

"I know this is hard, but that's why it's great.

"And I know you have a family, Matt, but bearing a mess with you might be their way to be great."

Matt was sitting very still. Inside he was very disturbed.

"But," Father Mike now said, "God also knows we are not God. God knows that no one has grown into all the sureness and strength that sometimes he needs in order to do things that most people would never even consider. I myself know that sometimes I have to ask people for something that they just cannot do."

Matt was still sitting without moving.

"And that's why there is mercy," said Father Mike. "If you are not able to risk turning these people in right now, then you are able to ask God to look at you with mercy. Maybe someday, maybe someday soon, things will change; and as soon as you see that they have, you can do something that will let you have more peace and pride. But right now, if this is not possible—this is your decision in conscience—if you don't *yet* have it in you to make a leap, you can accept God's love and mercy and patience."

"Are you telling me it's okay to do nothing?"

"No," said Father Mike, "I'm not telling you it's okay. I'm acknowledging that we have a really tough situation here, and God will be patient with you until we can resolve it.

"But I also talked to you about the response of 'greatness.' I am not helping you if I do not say this. I don't know if you have it in you *yet*, but you do need to know that doing something about this mess *is* greatness, and it is worth whatever you might pay, no matter what.

"Until then, you can count on God's mercy, and even if you won't feel perfect peace with things, you can still feel God's understanding and love.

"But there is," added Father Mike, "one thing you *can* do that you will need to do. If you are going to accept mercy from God for doing less than you 'should,' this means that you owe mercy to others around you who are going to do less than they should as you see it. Try to be compassionate to their humanity, and you will understand better how God is compassionate with yours. And don't worry, you'll get plenty of opportunity!"

Finally Matt was able to smile.

"One more thing," said Father Mike, "maybe I can anticipate something that might already be bothering you."

Father Mike paused in order to offer a smile of his own. "I know that having to deal with all this must seem very unfair. I mean, this is not one of those times that a person is suffering the consequences of something he chose to do, that he knew was wrong. I know you didn't ask for this, none of it.

"But God chooses some people for greatness. He knows what He's doing, and all of us will be richer forever *because* of what He's doing. The only question is: Are you one of the people God has chosen for greatness? This one is up to you."

Matt rose to leave, with a little—just a little—more spring in his step. ■

PART II:
WHY DO WE DO
THINGS DIFFERENTLY?

◘

WHY WE DO THINGS DIFFERENTLY
(FATHER MIKE EXPLAINS)

This Sunday was different. Father Mike had been hearing not grumbling but a lot of "observing" that here in their church, things were done differently than in other local churches. People were aware of this. Almost all were happy about it; but perhaps they would be even happier if they had a better explanation of how their church was different—and why.

This was the intro to his talk; after it, he got into specifics.

"The first way our church is different," he said, "and the most important way, is doctrine, or more exactly, the way we try to teach. Here we try to do what is now absolutely necessary: to explain things so that you can see the truth of it for yourself. This is called apologetics," explained Father Mike, "from the Greek word for 'explanation'; and it *is* absolutely necessary.

"You know perfectly well that you hear many different ideas. And everybody who talks to you is sure that he's right. But they say opposing things!

"Besides this ... you know that you *don't* know what really happened two thousand years ago. You know what the Bible says. But you also know that the Bible was written a long time ago; and it says some things that we don't believe any more *just as they are written*—like when it talks about Adam and Eve and Noah's Ark, and the damnation of everyone who isn't baptized! You know that other people out there quote the Bible in support of the damnation of everybody except them—and you're not very impressed with religious minds of those people! You know that every religion has its holy book that was written a long time ago, which says all kinds of fantastic things that we have no problem not believing. You know that ancient people explained things with stories we have no reason to accept. But," said Father Mike, "I'm sure you've wondered, how are our stories any different?"

Some people's faces showed that they had indeed wondered about this.

"No," continued Father Mike, "there is no way we can be sure enough about faith, so that it will really affect how we see everything, unless we can see the truth of it for ourselves.

"How else could we be sure enough that we were made for life with God so that when someone we love dies, we are still at peace?

"How else can we be sure enough that love is the way to a richer life with God so that if we are called upon to make a big sacrifice, we can do it?

"How else can we be sure enough that our lives really do follow God's plan, right down to the smallest detail, so that we can ... not only keep our peace when hard things happen ... but believe in ourselves for who we are so far, even though we live in a world where hardly anybody helps us do this, and many, many people have more than we do?

"By the way," added Father Mike, "right now, I am not just talking about apologetics, I am practicing it. Apologetics means we talk primarily about 'the basics'—heaven, love, and God's plan—so that we are constantly offering 'the gifts of faith'—those effects on our spirit that always follow if we really believe the basics. Here I am talking about peace and joy and a life that means something."

Those subjects were, indeed, what Father Mike always talked about.

He continued. "This way, faith inspires love, the way it's supposed to," he said. "You realize that God's plan for everything is also God's plan for you ... His plan to make you into someone He knows He can love with all His heart, forever. This allows you to love yourself—to be thrilled that you are you—and this allows you see the goodness in others so you can love them. You are *inspired* to love because you understand that love is the way to a richer life forever. You understand that by growing in love and helping others do the same, you are working for a richer life with God that all of us will share—and that doing this is the purpose of life here.

"Apologetics lets us keep things simple. And this affects the way we do things, and especially the way we celebrate Mass.

"Among the many bad things that have happened as faith has declined in our times," continued Father Mike, "is that religious talk makes no sense to most people, and religious actions look like somebody else's silly rituals. Here we are trying to break this down. I hope you've noticed that our ceremonies here are simpler, and it is usually pretty clear what they mean."

For sure, people had noticed that the ceremonies in their church were simpler.

Father Mike continued. "This is called 'transparency.' The actual goal is to do things so that even a person who has never been in church before can come and not feel strange, and instead feel that he or she understands what we are doing—and likes it!

This is also the reason that I comment so often on what Mass is, and how it works—how it represents the Last Supper, which is where Jesus really accepted the Cross, which was planned by God as *the* way to show us that He could not love us more!"

All these points were familiar.

Father Mike continued. "Also, apologetics lets us make instruction simpler. Let's face it: the basics are not hard to learn. This doesn't mean that we think we can teach people to be great Christians in six weeks. But people are supposed to grow into seeing the truth— into knowing God—all the days of their lives. Six weeks *is* enough to get them started. That's why you hear about how making your sacraments is so much 'easier' here. We're not trying to make it 'easy'; we're trying to get it done—to reach lots of people and to give them a reasonable chance of starting on the road to a deep faith. "And," added Father Mike, "the more people who are 'in' it, the more people who 'make it.'

"Now," said Father Mike with a slight change of tone, "as long as we are on the topic of sacraments, I'd like to say a quick word about marriage. I know that you know that we have many people among us who, perhaps, would not feel comfortable going to Communion if they had approached the Church somewhere else. We, here, have been perhaps more willing than other places at getting people to seek forgiveness for their part of a failed first marriage, and to have help to know whether the life they now share with someone one is an honest commitment as God sees it. This process is necessarily private, and I cannot talk about what, in effect, are people's confessions—I would not even be comfortable giving examples for the fear that some couples might think I was talking about them! But I ask you to trust me and be compassionate to the people around you. You have heard me say many times that no sincere person needs feel excluded from Communion. Let me also say this: no insincere person has been welcomed back to Communion!"

This statement generated a variety of reactions.

"I'm almost done. As long as we are on the topic of marriage, I would like to say a quick word about our approach to moral matters in general. Just as we have apologetics in doctrine and transparency in ceremonies, we are striving for 'nuance' when it comes to moral matters.

"In times past, people saw things mostly in black and white. Actually, we can still see this today in some people, especially those who seem to think that every sin should send *somebody else* to hell."

This got a laugh.

Father Mike continued. "We understand where this came from. Not only were people somewhat less sophisticated in past centuries than we are now, but doctrine supported this idea specifically: Adam and Eve messed up everything by disobeying. The human family is damned. Life here is about trying to get saved. Just as we got damned by disobeying, we get saved by obeying. And obeying what? The rules—the rules just as they are given by the Great Lawgiver.

"Now we understand things a good deal better. Now we know that we are here not to get saved from damnation but to allow God in His goodness to give us more—to participate in our own creation. We do this by growing in the love that makes us more like God and prepares us to share His life more richly forever. Love, then, is the basic rule. And now we see that specific rules, meant to tell us what love wants us to do in specific kinds of situations, do not always need to be obeyed in a black-and-white way in order to make love grow. In fact, now we see that to insist that certain things are 'always and everywhere' bad or good can actually injure the cause of love in the world.

"We also see, by the way, that when we explain things in a black-and-white way, they often strike people as wrong. Whereas when we explain things with nuance, insisting on only those rules really required by the cause of love, our rules strike people as right; and we successfully challenge them to give their all.

"And one more thing," said Father Mike. "Did anybody notice that, even today, I still offered our basic explanation of life and also the gifts of faith?"

People nodded their heads. Father Mike smiled at them and wrapped up his sermon. ■

IMOGENE
(FATHER MIKE COMES FACE-TO-FACE WITH THE PROBLEM OF EVIL)

Father Mike was not expecting something like this. Oh sure, he knew he was going to the missions. And he knew that he was traveling to a place that had experienced a civil war. But things had calmed down, had they not? There'd be much he needed to learn, for sure. But he was not expecting anything like this.

Her name was Imogene, and she came to the house to speak to a priest. The real father of the house was away for the day, but Imogene, like many people there, spoke English and spoke it well, so she asked to speak with Father Mike. One could see immediately that Imogene was smart and, even more quickly, that she was missing an eye and a hand. She walked with a limp. She wanted to talk.

"We never had much," she said, "but the little we had, they took whenever they came through.

"Sometimes, because they didn't leave enough for the children to eat, we tried to hide some things—but if they found them, they beat everyone in the house. Everyone. Even the children.

"This went on for a long time. It was a bad life for us. Not just being hungry but being treated like we were animals, without respect. And being scared. Sometimes they would accuse us of hiding things, but we weren't, but they didn't believe us so they beat us anyway until they got tired of it.

"One time they came and you could see that they were especially angry. Most, I think, were drunk. They wanted more than we had, and they just didn't listen when we swore we had nothing else and begged them to believe us.

"But this time they didn't just beat us.

"Oh, they had used their guns before. They would shoot at our things. They would shoot at us— but miss.

"But this time was different.

"They yelled at the parents and told them to hand over what we didn't have or they would shoot the children. The children were crying and looking at us for help, but there was nothing we could do.

"Again we begged them to believe us. But they didn't listen, and they shot my little boy in the head.

"It was horrible to see what happened to his head, and I wanted to go to him but they wouldn't let me.

"Now they said we had more food than we needed—so where were we hiding it? All I could do was beg them to believe that we had nothing else and then they shot my daughter.

"Now my husband found the strength to break away from those who were holding him, and he hit one, and this made them really angry and they set about to torture him. It was the most terrible thing to see and to hear. First they went to hurt him in his private parts; they were kicking him, and then they used the butts of their guns, and then someone used a knife. He was screaming like I never heard him do before, but he couldn't help it, and, of course, I couldn't help him.

"It was sickening to see when they went for his eyes, and even his tongue; and then they threw him down and started kicking him in the head.

"I couldn't tell at what moment he died.

"And then they came at me.

"They said that if I didn't have anything to give them ... well, there was one thing I could give them. And you could see what they wanted me to do.

"I don't think I was being brave or righteous; I was just confused and so disturbed I couldn't do anything but cry.

"They threatened me, but I couldn't do anything but cry.

"One of them grabbed my hand and said 'use it,' and when I could not, he cut it with his knife.

"They threw me down and started kicking me, and that's when I lost my eye.

"I'm sure they were planning to kill me when someone yelled that the 'uniforms' were coming and so they ran, and I was found, and that's how I survived.

"I came to ask you, Father, how could God let this happen?"

Father Mike knew that he dare not think that *he* was the unlucky one in this situation. He knew that he did not have the option of platitudes about "mystery." Even though he had often insisted that theology should not be expected to make sense to someone in the midst of great suffering, Imogene was asking. She was speaking to him calmly. Faith must be able to speak for God—or it is nothing at all.

"Give me a moment so I can start breathing," said Father Mike, and he noticed that this got from Imogene a somehow beautiful smile.

"You must know that it is hard to talk about ideas when someone has suffered so terribly. But I will try.

"Can I start by saying that evil, even the ugliest evil that has ever been described to me in person, cannot mean that God is not good? Experience tells us that all things come from God; and this means that

God must be very great, greater even than the greatest thing our minds *created by Him* can imagine; and this means that God is very, very good.

"We can insist on this, even in the face of terrible evil, because we can imagine that terrible things can have a good purpose—they can lead to very, very good things, greater because of what we went through to get them. We can imagine this because we see it all the time. We see it when a problem leads to an invention, a tragedy leads us in a new direction, a struggle leads us to appreciate things better, things like that.

"Is it okay that I am talking to you this way?"

Imogene nodded yes. Father Mike went on.

"Now I know that what has happened to you was more terrible than anything you will get for it *here*. But nothing about God makes sense unless we were made for life in *heaven*. If death is the end, life is no good—for anyone. God could not have made us for less than life with Him—and your children and your husband have that life *now*.

"But since God has to be good, there has to be a good reason He asks us to live here and go through so much. And the reason is that He wants us to help Him make us. He knows—we know—that our lives with Him will be richer forever if *we* help Him make *us* the people we will be.

"This means creating good. This means growing out the opposite of good, what we call 'evil.'

"This is why evil is possible. This is why evil is all around us, why evil is *in* us, in our ignorance and selfishness, and in our not-yet-perfect nature that can be confused and twisted, and filled with hatred and cruelty.

"This happens to some of us in God's family. We cause lots of trouble; we cause lots of pain. But God wants our love for our family to be greater than our worst problems. He is asking for special love for those who need it most—those who need help, those who need forgiveness, those who need mercy, more mercy than they will ever give to others *here*.

"And I know this must be hard for you to hear, Imogene, but even those monsters were once someone's babies. I don't know who *didn't* help them know better right from wrong. I don't know what happened in their lives that filled them with such anger. But I do know that this kind of evil is something that God's family has to conquer, and it is something we are going to conquer—even if we still have a long, long way to go.

"But we have already come a long way, Imogene. Not that long ago, most people would not have thought twice about what happened to you, much less ask how God could let this happen.

"When love finally conquers—and love *will* conquer, not hatred, not vengeance, but love—God will have a glorious people, more glorious for how far we've come.

"And to you, Imogene, I have to say this: You have been through so very much. In your own body you bear the cost of our future glory, and for you there will be special glory forever. That's part of the answer to what must be your question, Imogene, 'Why me?' God needed you to play this part in giving all He can to His family.

"God is good, and He has not asked you to bear what you've been through for nothing. You can know that one day you will see what has come from your suffering and you will rejoice in it. With your children and your husband. You will understand what, exactly, God was doing. He will answer your question better than I did.

"Have I said too much?"

Imogene shook her head.

"Then I need you to know one more thing. God knows, Imogene, what you've been through. And He has suffered with you, even more than a parent suffers the pain of her children. He felt what you went through as if it were Him. His knowledge of what we feel, and His love for us, let Him do no less. This is what He was trying to say with Jesus' agony on the Cross.

"And please forgive me for saying this: from that same Cross, Jesus said, 'Father, forgive them, for they know not what they do.'"

Imogene thought about that for a very long few seconds. Then she asked, "But why did it have to be so terrible?"

Now it was Father Mike who needed a few seconds.

He thought about his stock, correct answer.

Life has to be imperfect because if we were made perfect we would already be all we can be and we could not participate in making us, us.

Imperfection has to involve suffering—how else is it something bad that we are called to conquer?

Sometimes our suffering has to be terrible because our experience here has to be "real," and this means that when we are doing well, life has to be experienced as good; and when we are doing badly, life has to be experienced as bad—sometimes very bad.

He decided instead to say this: "To make you a queen forever for your courage and for your love." ■

◘

EPILOGUE

"T he Four Pillars" you read about is available in a full-page version. Just visit the author's website at www.thefaithkit.org and click on the actual Faith Kit.

Almost certainly you noticed that Father Mike gave one of his visitors a guide to spiritual reading; and two of his visitors received something he called a guide to theological reading. This material is also available to you. For the guide to spiritual reading, just go to thefaithkit.org and click on "How to Use This Site." For the guide to theological reading, visit this same website and click on "Visit Panorama." Then click on "Visit Panorama 2," and then click on the letter "Above Brooklyn."

The Faith Kit also offers a full-page version of the "My Bible Bookmark" that Father Mike gave Jerome. There you will also find "A New Way to Say the Rosary," which makes use of the new Hail Mary that Father Mike gave Margaret. The Faith Kit contains numerous items to help you keep faith in front of you.

Donna came back. She had more questions about other moral issues. Toward the end of her meeting with Father Mike, she mentioned a young person in her family who had confided in her that he was struggling with the issue of his sexuality. She did not imagine that he would be comfortable coming in for an appointment. Father Mike suggested that Donna go to thefaithkit.org/panorama, scroll down and click on the "Mini-Books" menu, and download "A Young Person's Guide to Sexual Honesty."

He suggested that Matt go to thefaithkit.org/panorama and download the "Letters to Theophilus." Father Mike assured Matt, "You'll recognize the letter that applies to you."

Finally, to "hear" more of Father Mike's homilies, go back to thefaithkit.org/panorama and take a look at the spiritual novel *Kirk*. ■

ABOUT THE AUTHOR

A priest of the Archdiocese of Newark, NJ, Robert J. Cormier was a preacher, teacher, theologian, and pilot.

For seventeen years, he led the Spanish-speaking community of St. Rose of Lima in Newark, a city he served for twenty-five years. During this time, he ministered ten years to Portuguese-speaking communities and one year to an Italian-speaking community.

In addition, Father Bob had over twenty-five years' experience in both elementary and high schools, and over twenty years as both a prison chaplain and a rehab counselor. For the last eighteen years of his life, he had been president of Project Live—a leading institution for the care of the mentally ill.

Between 1989 and 1998, he was one of the three voices of *The Radio Mass*, once heard live throughout the Eastern seaboard. He served as the spiritual director of the Internet-based radio station Radio Inmaculada, on which he also aired a weekly program.

Father Bob had a pontifical license in philosophy from the Catholic University of America in Washington, DC, and a license in theology from the Gregorian University in Rome. He was ordained by Pope John Paul II in 1982.

He served as a deacon in Thailand, visited some seventy other countries on six continents, and had some facility in eight modern languages. He spent fifteen summers as priest to the Mam, a Mayan tribe, in western Guatemala.

He was the creator of Christian Materialism, a strikingly new synthesis of philosophy and faith that comes complete with a spirituality, set of catechisms, books on marriage and ministry, works of fiction, music, and art, and more.

The combined tables of contents of his books and other writings and the catalog of his religious products include over two hundred pages.

Father Bob grew up in Cranford, NJ. Besides being a pilot, he was a mountain climber, sailor, cave explorer, scuba diver, and bus driver, and he played the conga.

He was a member of the pastoral team that serves St. Patrick and Assumption/All Saints parishes in Jersey City.

Father Robert J. Cormier died in a climbing accident on Mount Hood in Oregon in 2014, after reaching the summit.

ABOUT THE PUBLISHER

The Crossroad Publishing Company publishes CROSSROAD and HERDER & HERDER books. We offer a 200-year global family tradition of books on spiritual living and religious thought. We promote reading as a time-tested discipline for focus and understanding. We help authors shape, clarify, write and effectively promote their ideas. We select, edit, and distribute books. Our expertise and passion is to provide wholesome spiritual nourishment for heart, mind and soul through the written word.

You Might Also Like

Robert J. Cormier

Better Than We Believed
How to Apply the Vision That Is Faith
to the Struggle That Is Life

Recipient of the Eric Hoffer Award

Paperback, 192 pages, ISBN 978-0-8245-4980-0

Presuming nothing that both traditional believers and critical-thinking searchers will not find in their hearts, *Better Than We Believed* presents a strikingly clear concept of faith that answers the questions of people you will recognize:

- MARK who struggles with anger
- IRENE who battles stress
- HENRY who is consumed by hatred
- GLORIA who has been betrayed
- MARY who feels trapped
- JOY who can't get over death
- JAMES who is dying

As we witness this faith applied to these and other serious struggles, we will see it can transform our experience, and offer us peace, purpose, and joy.

Please support your local bookstore or order directly from the
publisher at www.crossroadpublishing.com

To request a catalog or inquire about
quantity orders, please e-mail
sales@CrossroadPublishing.com .

✝ The Crossroad Publishing Company

You Might Also Like

Robert J. Cormier

Why We Look Up
Making Sense of Our Catholic Faith

Paperback, 144 pages, ISBN 978-0-8245-2120-2

People who want to understand what they believe will cherish these inspiring reflections—which offer proof that you don't need to be a theologian to have a rich faith that nourishes the heart and mind.

In the book's three parts, "Having Faith," "Living Faith," and "Practicing Faith," the award-winning author provides us with small gems for devotional reading and inspiration, on a wealth of questions that matter to us most, such as what suffering means, how to have a personal relationship with God, and the glory of Creation.

"Robert Cormier is a superb communicator. He makes faith come alive in words that people can understand. He makes you want a life of faith, and he shows you how to find it."

—Rev. Arthur Caliandro
Marble Collegiate Church, New York

Please support your local bookstore or order directly from the publisher at www.crossroadpublishing.com

*To request a catalog or inquire about
quantity orders, please e-mail
sales@CrossroadPublishing.com*

✝ The Crossroad Publishing Company

You Might Also Like

Robert J. Cormier

A Faith That Makes Sense
Reflections for Peace, Purpose, and Joy

Hardcover, 240 pages, ISBN 978-0-8245-1875-2

In this collection of brief reflections, Father Cormier takes elements common to many faiths and offers them in a way that can make sense to almost everyone. The simplicity and clarity of the reflections makes the texts easily accessible to a wide variety of readers. If read slowly and over time, they can inspire serious meditations.

"Written for those searching for faith, or those hoping to understand their faith more deeply, *A Faith That Makes Sense* takes the reader on a simple and optimistic journey. 'Share what faith has done for you,' we are urged. Robert Cormier takes his own advice and spells out what love, peace, and joy—as well as prayer, struggle, sacrifice, and so much more—amounts to, if understood in light of a faith made eminently sensible, and readable, in this insightful book."

—Rev. Dr. Paul A. Holmes, director
Toolbox for Pastoral Management, Seton Hall University

Please support your local bookstore or order directly from the publisher at www.crossroadpublishing.com

*To request a catalog or inquire about
quantity orders, please e-mail
sales@CrossroadPublishing.com*

The Crossroad Publishing Company

You Might Also Like

Maria Boulding, OSB

Gateway to Hope
An Exploration of Failure

Paperback, 160 pages, ISBN 978-0-8245-2698-6

With each passage embracing human failure and loss, the elegant musings of Sister Maria Boulding speak gently and eloquently to those who set their goals high, yet struggle to grasp their own limitations and reconcile them with God, as well as to those who second guess their path in life, and to worshipers mourning the premature loss of friends and family. With each meditation on loss, Sister Boulding creates a spiritual, contemplative grid against which readers can interpret the setbacks of their life.

"[A] wonderful portrait of many failures throughout Scripture and how we all go through life dealing with the fear of failure and failure, itself. However, Boulding stresses that it is in failing that we come to realize how we can become successful."

—Rev. John Hogemann, OSB

Please support your local bookstore or order directly from the publisher at www.crossroadpublishing.com

*To request a catalog or inquire about
quantity orders, please e-mail
sales@CrossroadPublishing.com*

The Crossroad Publishing Company